Business Machines Incorporated

v.

Minicom Incorporated

Tenth Edition

Faculty Materials

Business Machines Incorporated

v.

Minicom Incorporated

Tenth Edition

Faculty Materials

Anthony J. Bocchino

Donald H. Beskind

National Institute for Trial Advocacy

Address inquiries to:

Reprint Permission
National Institute for Trial Advocacy
1685 38th Street, Suite 200
Boulder, CO 80301-2735
Phone: (800) 225-6482
Fax: (720) 890-7069
E-mail: permissions@nita.org

ISBN 978-1-60156-394-1
FBA 1394

Printed in the United States of America

CONTENTS

National Institute for Trial Advocacy

INTRODUCTION

This is a contract action between Business Machines Inc. (BMI), the plaintiff, and Minicom Inc., the defendant. BMI claims that it entered into a contract to sell 100 gross of integrated chip platforms (known as ICP-73s) to Minicom for $500,000, plus shipping costs. BMI asserts that the parts were shipped to Minicom by National Parcel Service (NPS) and the shipment was lost while it was in the possession of NPS. It is BMI's position that once the goods were delivered to NPS, BMI had complied with its contractual obligations and the risk of loss had transferred to Minicom. BMI is claiming that Minicom, by failing to pay for the parts, breached the contract and is seeking damages in the amount of $500,000, plus interest and shipping costs. Minicom defends by saying that the contract included a term requiring BMI to insure the shipment of ICP-73s. Minicom claims that the term was agreed to in one or some combination of the following ways:

1. Michael Lubell and Virginia Young, as agents of Minicom and BMI, respectively, entered into a verbal contract that required BMI to ship the goods insured for full value.

2. Michael Lubell and Virginia Young had a conversation in which Lubell told Young that he wanted to buy the goods and have them shipped fully insured. Ms. Young told him that was acceptable and to confirm this request in an order by fax or letter, which he did. Both of these acts were within the scope of her agency. Lubell sent an order by fax, followed by a letter, that incorporated the conversation.

3. Michael Lubell sent an order by fax followed by a letter that made reference to the prior course of dealing between the parties (the only prior shipment in September of YR-2 that had been sent insured), and he asked that the new transaction be handled per the same agreement.

Minicom has filed a counterclaim for past and future losses.

Minicom asserts that BMI's failure to insure the shipment of ICPs breached the contract and forced Minicom to purchase cover goods at a cost of $50,000 over the original contract price. Minicom also alleges that BMI's failure to deliver the ICPs cost Minicom a contract that would have resulted in a profit of $100,000. Minicom alleges that it also lost future profits.

BMI replied to Minicom's counterclaim by alleging that Minicom failed to mitigate its damages. BMI also denied Virginia Young was its agent for purposes of contracting with Lubell and Minicom.

Pretrial discovery has been completed. The applicable law is contained in the Pretrial Rulings and in the Proposed Jury Instructions.

All of the witness roles in this case file may be played by either a woman or a man. The facts should be altered to be consistent with the witness.

All dates are stated in the "year minus" (YR-) format. To use an actual date in testimony or otherwise simply subtract the number shown after the minus sign from the current year. For example, in 2014, YR-1 is 2013 (or last year), YR-2 is 2012 (two years ago), and YR-10 is 2004 (ten years ago.

For exhibits with a "Received" stamp on them, those documents are the copies produced by the recipient during discovery and those stamps were placed by the appropriate person at the recipient's place of business. The senders of the documents have copies of these documents that had been produced without the "received" demarcation. Those exhibits are omitted from this file for space considerations.

STIPULATIONS AND PRETRIAL RULINGS

Stipulations

1. All the documents in the case file are "authentic" within the meaning of Article 9 of the Federal Rules of Evidence, are what they purport to be, and comply with the "original documents rule" within the meaning of Article 10 of the Federal Rules of Evidence.

2. BMI and Minicom have had two agreements regarding the purchase of electronic parts, the first in September of YR-2 and the second in January of YR-1.

3. Minicom had a contract to provide 5,000 handheld wearable computers (HWCs) to Neiman Marcus that provided if the original order performed technically as promised, a second order of 15,000 units would be made and shipped for October 1, YR-1, delivery.

    The original 5,000 unit shipment was to be delivered to Neiman Marcus no later than April 1, YR-1. When Minicom was unable to meet that delivery deadline, the order was cancelled by Neiman Marcus pursuant to the terms of the contract between Neiman Marcus and Minicom. There was no other binding contract between Neiman Marcus and Minicom for orders after the 5,000 unit order of April YR-1. However the parties contemplated purchase by Nieman Marcus of an additional 15,000 units in October of YR-2 and an additional two years of 20,000 units per year assuming Minicom's HWC's remained technically up-to-date.

4. If called to testify, Neiman Marcus manager Greg Smith would say he told Elliot Milstein that assuming the HWCs performed according to their description an additional 15,000 units would be ordered for October 1, YR-1, delivery and that if Minicom kept up with technical advances, Minicom could expect orders of approximately 20,000 units per year beginning in YR-0. Mr. Smith would also testify that after cancelling the Minicom order, Neiman Marcus made a three-year commitment to another supplier of HWCs.

5. The calendar included in this file is the accurate calendar for the time periods shown on it.

Pretrial Rulings

1. The risk of loss for the shipment of ICP-73s from BMI to Minicom in January of YR-1 passed from BMI to Minicom when the ICP-73s were delivered by BMI to NPS. This ruling is consistent with established Nita law and will not be reconsidered.

2. Parol evidence concerning the contract between BMI and Minicom for the purchase of ICP-73s in January YR-1 will be permitted.

~ YR-2 ~

September

Su	M	T	W	Th	F	Sa
1	2	3	4	5	6	7
8	9	10	11	12	13	14
15	16	17	18	19	20	21
22	23	24	25	26	27	28
29	30					

October

Su	M	T	W	Th	F	Sa
		1	2	3	4	5
6	7	8	9	10	11	12
13	14	15	16	17	18	19
20	21	22	23	24	25	26
27	28	29	30	31		

November

Su	M	T	W	Th	F	Sa
					1	2
3	4	5	6	7	8	9
10	11	12	13	14	15	16
17	18	19	20	21	22	23
24	25	26	27	28	29	30

December

Su	M	T	W	Th	F	Sa
1	2	3	4	5	6	7
8	9	10	11	12	13	14
15	16	17	18	19	20	21
22	23	24	25	26	27	28
29	30	31				

~ YR-1 ~

January

Su	M	T	W	Th	F	Sa
			1	2	3	4
5	6	7	8	9	10	11
12	13	14	15	16	17	18
19	20	21	22	23	24	25
26	27	28	29	30	31	

February

Su	M	T	W	Th	F	Sa
						1
2	3	4	5	6	7	8
9	10	11	12	13	14	15
16	17	18	19	20	21	22
23	24	25	26	27	28	

March

Su	M	T	W	Th	F	Sa
						1
2	3	4	5	6	7	8
9	10	11	12	13	14	15
16	17	18	19	20	21	22
23	24	25	26	27	28	29
30	31					

April

Su	M	T	W	Th	F	Sa
		1	2	3	4	5
6	7	8	9	10	11	12
13	14	15	16	17	18	19
20	21	22	23	24	25	26
27	28	29	30			

May

Su	M	T	W	Th	F	Sa
				1	2	3
4	5	6	7	8	9	10
11	12	13	14	15	16	17
18	19	20	21	22	23	24
25	26	27	28	29	30	31

June

Su	M	T	W	Th	F	Sa
1	2	3	4	5	6	7
8	9	10	11	12	13	14
15	16	17	18	19	20	21
22	23	24	25	26	27	28
29	30					

Materials Available to All Sides

IN THE SUPERIOR COURT

IN AND FOR THE COUNTY OF DARROW AND STATE OF NITA

BUSINESS MACHINES INCORPORATED,	)	
	)	
Plaintiff,	)	CIVIL ACTION
	)	YR-1:2342
v.	)	
	)	
MINICOM INCORPORATED,	)	COMPLAINT
	)	
Defendant.	)	

The plaintiff for its complaint against the defendant alleges:

1. At all relevant times, the defendant, Minicom Incorporated (hereinafter Minicom), was a Nita corporation authorized to do business within the State of Nita and having an office and principal place of business located at 724 Science Drive in Nita City, County of Darrow and State of Nita.

2. At all relevant times, Minicom was in the business of designing, manufacturing, selling, and distributing computers known in the trade as handheld wearable computers.

3. At all relevant times, the plaintiff, Business Machines Incorporated (hereinafter BMI) was a Delaware corporation, maintaining a place of business at One Industrial Drive in Brookline, Massachusetts.

4. At all relevant times, BMI was in the business of manufacturing, selling, and distributing office equipment, computers, software, and electronic and mechanical computer parts.

5. At all relevant times, Elliot Milstein and Michael Lubell were employees and agents of Minicom and held themselves out to BMI as such.

6. On or about January 6, YR-1, Michael Lubell sent a letter by facsimile and USPS to BMI's Brookline, Massachusetts, sales office and ordered 100 gross of integrated chip platforms, which are electronic devices containing operating instructions for small computers. These parts are designated ICP-73 in BMI's catalog and price list. The terms of the sale were payment of the full purchase price of $500,000 within sixty days of delivery except that a credit of 2 percent was to be given for payment within thirty days of delivery and a service charge of 1.5 percent per month was to be added to any balance still outstanding sixty days after delivery.

7. On or about January 17, YR-1, BMI delivered to National Parcel Service (hereinafter NPS) for shipment to Minicom four parcels, each containing twenty-five gross of ICP-73s.

8. On or about January 27, YR-1, Minicom notified BMI that the shipment had not been received and BMI notified NPS and directed NPS to trace the missing parcels.

9. On or about February 14, YR-1, NPS informed BMI that the goods had been lost in transit. BMI received a check from NPS in the amount of $400.00, which represented NPS's maximum liability in the absence of declared excess valuation or insurance.

10. On or about February 14, YR-1, BMI notified Minicom that the shipment had been lost and forwarded NPS's check to Minicom with the following endorsement: "Pay to the order of Minicom Incorporated."

11. On or about March 3, YR-1, BMI sent a letter to Minicom demanding payment for the goods delivered to NPS for shipment to Minicom. As of the date of this action, no payment has been received.

WHEREFORE, the plaintiff prays for

1. $500,122.60 in compensatory damages;

2. interest as provided by the agreement between the parties; and

3. such other relief as the court deems just and proper.

JURY DEMAND

Plaintiff demands a trial by jury in this action.

NORRIS, KROLL & SIMON by:

Elizabeth Simon

Elizabeth Simon
One Hancock Place
Boston, Massachusetts 01771
(617) 872-9331
Attorney for Plaintiff

DATED: May 9, YR-1

RETURN ON SUMMONS

I hereby certify that on May 13, YR-1, the above complaint and the summons were personally served on Charles A. Horton III, attorney for Minicom Inc., in his office at Suite 400, First National Bank Building, Nita City, Nita.

James Bell

James Bell

Speedy Summons & Process Inc.

IN THE SUPERIOR COURT

IN AND FOR THE COUNTY OF DARROW AND STATE OF NITA

BUSINESS MACHINES INCORPORATED,   )
)
Plaintiff   )   CIVIL ACTION Plaintiff,
)   YR-1:2342
v.   )
)   ANSWER AND
MINICOM INCORPORATED,   )   COUNTERCLAIM
)
Defendant.   )

ANSWER

1. Paragraphs 1, 2, 3, 4, 5, 7, 10, and 11 are admitted.

2. As to Paragraphs 6, it is admitted that Minicom ordered 100 gross of ICP-73s at a price of $500,000. In all other respects, Paragraph 6 is denied. By way of further response, Minicom also sent its order letter to BMI by USPS.

3. As to Paragraphs 8 and 9, the defendant has insufficient information or knowledge on which to form a belief and so leaves the plaintiff to its proof of the matters therein alleged.

COUNTERCLAIM

1. At all relevant times, Chris Kay and Virginia Young were employees and agents of Business Machines Inc. (hereinafter BMI) and held themselves out to Minicom Inc. (hereinafter Minicom) as such.

2. Before the transaction described in the plaintiff's complaint, on or about September 3, YR-2, Minicom purchased from BMI 100 gross of BMI's part number ICP-73, an electronic device used in small computers. Under the terms of the agreement, BMI agreed to ship the goods via National Parcel Service (hereinafter NPS) and insure them for their full value. Minicom agreed to pay all shipping and insurance costs.

3. On or about September 6, YR-2, BMI delivered the shipment to NPS for delivery to Minicom. BMI declared excess valuation of $500,000 and prepaid shipping and insurance charges.

4. On or about September 10, YR-2, the shipment was received by Minicom.

5. On or about September 23, YR-2, Minicom paid BMI $491,232.60, the total purchase price of the goods, less a 2 percent discount for prompt payment, plus shipping and insurance charges.

6. On or about January 6, YR-1, Michael Lubell, Vice President for Purchasing at Minicom, telephoned the office of Chris Kay at BMI's Brookline, Massachusetts, sales office. Virginia Young answered the phone and was told by Michael Lubell that Minicom was placing an order for 100 gross of ICP-73s at the same price and under the same shipping and insurance terms as the September transaction. Virginia Young agreed to leave a message for Chris Kay as to the substance of her conversation with Michael Lubell.

7. On or about January 6, YR-1, Michael Lubell sent by facsimile and USPS a letter to Chris Kay at BMI's sales office in Brookline, Massachusetts, confirming the telephone conversation described in Paragraph 6 and stating again that the transaction was to be on the same terms as the September 3, YR-2, purchase described in Paragraph 2. The letter called on Chris Kay to notify Michael Lubell immediately if a sale on the same terms as the September transaction was not acceptable to BMI. No such notification was received.

8. BMI shipped the ordered ICP 73s to Minicom via NPS without requesting or paying for additional insurance.

9. Minicom never received the goods it ordered from BMI on or about January 6, YR-1, because, on information and belief, NPS lost the shipment after receiving it from BMI.

10. On or about March 10, YR-1, after receiving notification from BMI that the shipment had been lost in transit and that BMI did not intend to send another replacement shipment unless the original shipment was paid for, Minicom ordered technically identical replacement ICPs from Exrox Incorporated. Those goods were delivered to Minicom on March 18, YR-1, at a cost of $550,000.

11. Between the date on which the shipment from BMI was due to be received, which was on or about January 27, YR-1, and the date on which substitute goods were delivered, which was March 18, YR-1, Minicom was unable to produce certain types of microcomputers and, as a result, lost net profits.

WHEREFORE, the defendant prays for

1. $150,000 in compensatory damages;

2. past and future lost profits;

3. interest as provided by law; and

4. such other and further relief as is just and proper.

JURY DEMAND

Defendant demands a trial by jury in this action.

HORTON, STEIN & BENSON

Attorney for Defendant by:

Charles A. Horton

Charles A. Horton III
Suite 400
First National Bank Building
Nita City, Nita 80027
(720) 555-6464

DATED: June 2, YR-1

IN THE SUPERIOR COURT

IN AND FOR THE COUNTY OF DARROW AND STATE OF NITA

BUSINESS MACHINES INCORPORATED,	)	
	)	CIVIL ACTION
Plaintiff,	)	YR-1:2342
	)	
v.	)	
	)	REPLY TO
MINICOM INCORPORATED,	)	COUNTERCLAIM
	)	
Defendant.	)	

1. Paragraph 1 is admitted as to Chris Kay. It is admitted as to Virginia Young, except as it relates to the acceptance of contracts.

2. Paragraphs 2, 3, 4, 5, 8, and 9 are admitted.

3. Paragraphs 6 and 7 are denied.

4. As to Paragraphs 10 and 11, the plaintiff has insufficient information on which to form a belief as to the truth or falsity of said statements and therefore denies them.

AFFIRMATIVE DEFENSE

1. In failing to timely purchase replacement goods for those lost by NPS, Minicom failed to mitigate its damages.

NORRIS, KROLL & SIMON by:

Elizabeth Simon

Elizabeth Simon
One Hancock Place
Boston, Massachusetts 01771
(617) 872-9331
Attorney for Plaintiff

DATED: June 16, YR-1

IN THE SUPERIOR COURT

IN AND FOR THE COUNTY OF DARROW AND STATE OF NITA

BUSINESS MACHINES INCORPORATED,	)	
	)	CIVIL ACTION
Plaintiff,	)	YR-1:2342
	)	
v.	)	
	)	REQUEST FOR
MINICOM INCORPORATED,	)	ADMISSION
	)	
Defendant.	)	

As permitted by the Rules of Civil Procedure, plaintiff requests that the defendant admit the following:

1. Within the business and trade of which Minicom and BMI are parties, it is the normal custom and practice of companies shipping goods to ship them prepaid, without insuring them or declaring excess valuation, unless specifically requested to do so by agreement with the person to whom the goods are to be delivered or by some other person with an insurable interest in the goods.

NORRIS, KROLL & SIMON by:

Elizabeth Simon
One Hancock Place
Boston, Massachusetts 01771
(617) 872-9331
Attorney for Plaintiff

DATED: June 17, YR-1

IN THE SUPERIOR COURT

IN AND FOR THE COUNTY OF DARROW AND STATE OF NITA

BUSINESS MACHINES INCORPORATED,	)	
	)	CIVIL ACTION
Plaintiff,	)	YR-1:2342
	)	
v.	)	
	)	RESPONSE TO REQUEST
MINICOM INCORPORATED,	)	FOR ADMISSION
	)	
Defendant.	)	

Defendant responding to plaintiff's first request for admission admits the matter asserted. By way of further response, however, a specific agreement between Minicom and BMI required BMI to declare excess valuation and purchase full value insurance against loss or damage to the contents of the shipment.

HORTON, STEIN & BENSON by:

Charles A. Horton

Charles A. Horton III
Suite 400
First National Bank Building
Nita City, Nita 80027
(720) 555-6464
Attorney for Defendant

DATED: June 30, YR-1

Expert Report of Dr. Singell

An Evaluation of the Economic Loss to BMI from Failure of Minicom to Deliver on Contract

The purpose of this report is twofold:

1) to evaluate any economic loss caused to BMI by Minicom's failure to pay the contract price in its contract with BMI after BMI had met the contract's terms of delivery for 100 gross integrated chip platforms, and

2) to rebut the evaluation of the loss provided by Minicom's economist.

In performing this evaluation I have reviewed all of the pleadings in the case; all of the documents in the case marked as Exhibits 1–42; and the depositions of Kay, Young, Lubell, and Milstein. I have also reviewed the report of Dr. Seligman. All of this information has been provided by counsel for BMI. In brief, the facts are as follows.

BMI is in the business of manufacturing, selling, and distributing office equipment, computers, software, and electronic and mechanical computer parts.

In January of YR-1, BMI took an order from Minicom for 100 gross of integrated chip platforms. The terms of the sale were payment of full purchase price of $500,000 within sixty days of delivery, except that a credit of 2 percent was given for payment within thirty days of delivery and a service charge of 1.5 percent per month was added to any balance still outstanding sixty days after delivery.

This 100 gross of integrated chip platforms were produced by BMI and according to the contract shipped by National Parcel Service (NPS) in a timely manner. BMI takes the position that when these goods were put into the hands of NPS in a timely manner, and the parts were not insured because there was not a specific request to do so, BMI was in full compliance with its contractual obligation. These goods were lost in shipment with NPS, and BMI cannot, it is alleged, be held responsible for this failure. When informed by Minicom that the goods failed to arrive, BMI immediately contacted NPS. After an unsuccessful search for the merchandise, NPS provided BMI with a check for the maximum loss per package absent declaration of excess valuation. This check was forwarded immediately to Minicom with the endorsement "pay to the order of Minicom Inc." BMI alleges that it fulfilled the terms of the contract.

The economic analysis below assumes that BMI's allegations with regard to the interpretation of the contract are valid. Given this assumption, the economic loss to BMI resulted from the failure of Minicom to compensate BMI for its shipment. Furthermore, the contract specified interest associated with failure to pay the balance within sixty days of delivery. This loss may be summarized as follows:

Value of Loss	Description of Loss
$500,123	Full price specified in contract for 100 gross of integrated chip platforms plus shipping cost.
$112,528	1.5 percent per month after sixty days from delivery.
$612,651	Total Economic Loss

Finally, at the request of counsel, I have been asked to review the findings of "An Evaluation of the Economic Loss to Minicom Inc. from the Failure of BMI to Deliver on Contract," filed by Minicom's economist. I have carefully reviewed this report and offer the following observations:

1) BMI alleges that it fulfilled its contractual obligations by delivering the 100 gross of integrated computer platforms to NPS in a timely manner. Furthermore, it notified NPS and Minicom of the loss in a prudent manner and forwarded the NPS check to Minicom. If BMI has in fact fulfilled this contract, the analysis provided by Minicom's economist is not relevant and does not identify the relevant economic loss.

2) BMI further alleges that if Minicom had, as agreed, paid them for the shipment of goods, they would have provided a replacement order at the listed price in their existing contract. Hence, the additional $50,000 cost, which Minicom incurred for the purchase of cover goods, would not have been necessary if they had honored the contract.

3) Minicom also had the opportunity to purchase integrated computer platforms in the open market. Indeed, there are a number of suppliers, and this market is highly competitive. Furthermore, Minicom should have been motivated to mitigate its damage by seeking these alternative sources of supply if they chose not to deal with BMI. Therefore, BMI should not be held liable for the economic loss that resulted from Minicom's failure to mitigate damages.

4) While, as described above, this may not be relevant, questions may also be raised regarding the assumptions made by the economist for Minicom with respect to the discount rate, direct and indirect losses in profits, and, therefore, the evaluation of the economic loss presented in this report. In sum, from an economic point of view, if, as alleged, BMI honored the contract by the delivery of 100 gross of integrated platforms to the shipping company, they are entitled to recover the contract price, shipping cost, and specified late interest charges as specified in the contract from Minicom. In general, therefore, the economic analysis of the loss provided by Minicom's economist seems irrelevant. Nevertheless, it may be appropriate to point out that a number of the assumptions made in the evaluation of the loss are not consistent with the normal practices of economists in evaluating such losses. In particular,

   a. If Minicom had honored the contract by paying BMI for the delivery, BMI would have provided replacement parts at the agreed price of $500,000. Thus, Minicom would not have had to pay $50,000 more for parts.

   b. This discount rate of 8.5 percent is inappropriate because it does not incorporate the high risks associated with start-up enterprises or businesses currently operating in the computer field. A rate of 25 to 30 percent is typically used in such situations.

   c. The evaluation of the indirect loss may be inappropriate. Minicom's own business plans forecast growth in their output and sales over the future. This growth would lower unit costs as output expands and, thus, make these indirect profit losses irrelevant.

   d. Minicom does not present evidence to document that the lost sale to Nieman Marcus resulted exclusively from the late delivery. The national and regional economic slowdown could also explain a reduction in orders, and their economist does not consider this.

e. The economist for Minicom considers the possibility of losses continuing for a ten-year period. This seems unlikely given the rapid rate of technical change in this industry. Indeed, even a five-year period is excessive. The relevant loss would, given reasonable economic probabilities, be recovered in two years.

In summary, based on the above, in my opinion, and based on reasonable economic probabilities, the losses would be reduced at least in the following way:

PAST LOSS

The past loss would at most be $100,000, not $150,000, because the additional cost of $50,000 would not have occurred if Minicom had appropriately mitigated its losses.

FUTURE LOSS

At most, if Minicom can document that the loss in Nieman Marcus's order was the exclusive result of delayed product delivery brought about by the lost integrated chip platforms, the loss could be as high as the losses summarized in the following table (note: the present value of the loss is obtained using a discount rate of only 25 percent, and, as appropriate, the loss is considered for a maximum of only five years, although a loss for only two years seems probable. Also, as appropriate, no indirect profit loss is considered).

PAST LOSS TO MINICOM, INC.

Duration of Loss in Years	Value of Loss	Present Value of Loss
2	$800,000	$576,000
5	$2,000,000	$1,075,700

In conclusion, in my opinion, based on reasonable economic probabilities and given BMI's legal interpretation of the contract, BMI has suffered an economic loss of $612,651, and Minicom is due nothing. If BMI's interpretation of the contract is found invalid, there are a number of problems or errors in analysis in the economic evaluation of the loss presented by their expert. These errors result in the loss being overstated by millions of dollars. I would be willing to review additional information that may be forthcoming in your continued discovery and to provide my final evaluation of the loss to BMI for the court's consideration should this be necessary.

Larry D. Singell Sr.
Professor of Economics
Nita State University
September 15, YR-1
LDS/ss

Interview with Dr. Singell

October 20, YR -1

DR. SINGELL gave the following answers in an interview with the attorneys.

Dr. Singell began by corroborating the information on his résumé regarding qualifications as well as his Rule 26 disclosures regarding testimony within the last four years and publications within the past ten years. He then stated that he stood by the opinion contained in his report. In addition, Dr. Singell provided the following information.

Choice of Discount Rate

As background, it should be noted that the evaluation of the loss requires two separate steps. The first involves the evaluation of lost profits from the date of the alleged wrongdoing into the future. Lost profits are the difference between reasonably likely revenues and the reasonably likely cost associated with meeting the obligations under question. The result of this step is a year-by-year identification of lost profits from the date of injury until the alleged economic damage will end. The second step involves reducing these year-by-year profit losses to a present value. The present value is the amount of money, which, when prudently invested, will exactly replace the future lost profits. This reduction to present value is made by applying a discount rate, which the expert judges to be reasonably likely in similarly situated business decisions.

I chose a 25 percent discount rate in this case for determining the present value of Minicom's future economic losses of the Neiman Marcus account for the sale of the handheld wearable computers (HWC). The reason I chose the 25 percent discount rate is due to the high volatility of the computer industry and the startup nature of Minicom. The HWC product produced by Minicom is likely to be obsolete and will need to be replaced within one or two years. This would result in Minicom's loss of the market for their HWC. Minicom would either lose sales or be required to invest capital to change the HWC by producing newer and newer versions of the product to compete in the market. If the newer and newer versions were not produced, then Minicom would lose their share of the market without regard to the lost shipment of chip platforms.

Q: How did you choose the discount rate you used for your analysis?

A: In researching the appropriate discount rate in this case, I used standard and economic research principles.

Q: What were the research principles that you used?

A: I first looked at the United States Labor Department and Department of Commerce statistics to determine the behavior of the HWC portion of the computer industry market.

Q: Why did you look at the Department of Labor and Department of Commerce statistics first?

A: These statistical databases tend to be the most reliable and objective source when doing this type of research.

Q: What did you find in the labor and commerce statistics about the HWC markets?

A: I did not find this source to have any information about the industry, because the data in the USDL and DOC statistics were too aggregated to be helpful. The data did not meaningfully segregate out the HWC market data from the broader laptop and desktop computer market data.

Q: What did you research next?

A: Second, I researched data in trade publications and trade databases on the HWC market and found the information unreliable. This trade data is the second most reliable source for this type of research.

Q: What did you find on the HWC market in the trade journals?

A: Not much.

Q: Why weren't the trade journals helpful?

A: Unfortunately, for the HWC market, this trade data source is dominated by information from competitors in the market and just could not be considered reliable due to competition bias. The publications and the databases are produced by companies competing with one another for the HWC market and tend to exaggerate or minimize problems or withhold critical information of their economic position to protect their trade strategies and their trade secret information. Indeed, these trade documents are published by representatives of the industry who provide guarantees to their members against disclosure of critical information. However, information that was available showed some evidence of the HWC market.

Q: What did you find in the trade journals about the HWC market?

A: I found evidence of an unstable, quickly changing market structure characterized by broad fluctuations of demand for product and regular introduction of new technology.

Q: What else did you do in researching the discount rate?

A: Third in my standard economic analysis, I tried to analogize the HWC market to the market of a similar computer product. This is commonly recognized as the third most reliable source of information.

Q: Were you able to find an analogous product market?

A: No, this device was not very reliable in coming up with hard data on the HWC market. The diversity of the technology in the HWC market does not lend itself very well to analogies.

Q: What did you find?

A: What I was able to extrapolate from analogy to the small laptop market was that the HWC market continues to be marked by extreme volatility due to competition and technological advancements. Competitive strategies of computer equipment companies are cutthroat and are in constant flux, thus resulting in the need for a double-digit discount rate.

Q: What else did you do to research the appropriate discount rate for this case?

A: Finally, I resorted to what is commonly recognized in the economics world as the least reliable technique for finding market data on the HWC market trends. I asked BMI's lawyer to find me a reputable person in the computer industry to interview to try to get further information and data on the

HWC market. This method is highly subjective and can be influenced by the bias and prejudices of the person interviewed.

Q: Who did the BMI attorneys suggest that you interview about the HWC market?

A: I had a forty-five minute telephone conversation with Mr. Chris Kay at the time I was preparing my report in regard to the HWC market. He confirmed for me that the market was highly volatile due to ever-changing technology. This confirmed my need for a high discount rate.

Q: What else did you find that supports your opinion?

A: The 25 to 30 percent discount rate is also merited by the fact that Minicom is a start-up company.

Q: What is about Minicom as a start-up company that makes the 25 to 30 percent discount rate appropriate in your opinion?

A: Since they have no real long-term track record of sales of HWC products, projecting lost profits out into the future becomes highly speculative, thereby meriting the higher discount rate. The calculation of a discount rate for lost profits on the HWC is highly speculative anyway, because Mr. Kay told me (and I confirmed by looking at the documents) that there was no evidence of a Neiman Marcus contract in this case. Furthermore, the national and regional economic slowdown could be an explanation for the lost market for the HWC. Likewise, any calculation of indirect losses for selling to additional markets would be speculative. Since Minicom is a start-up, it is not relevant to consider the loss of reputation as a loss.

Q: What else did you consider?

A: In calculating the price of money in the short term, economic principles require a higher discount rate due to the unusually high uncertainty in the HWC market. This uncertainty results from the rapid technological innovation, wide fluctuations in demand, and Minicom's position as a start-up company. Furthermore, in short-run downturns in the economy (two years) people are most likely to do without handheld computer devices. The average of the broader economic cycles of the longer term (five to ten years) characterized by ups and downs in the market should not be used in this case due to the volatility of the market and Minicom's start-up status.

Q: How often have you used this high of a discount rate in calculating the time value of money?

A: I have rarely used a discount rate this high. I can think of only one case in my career where I chose 25 percent as a discount rate. That was in a situation similar to this one, involving a start-up company in a highly volatile sales market.

Q: What effect does this high of a discount rate have on projecting losses into the distant future?

A: I admit that as the term of the loss is projected further and further out, if the 25 percent discount rate is in error, the error becomes larger over time.

Q: What are the appropriate future loss time periods for Minicom, in your opinion?

A: As I stated in my report, I do not believe that it is appropriate to project Minicom's losses beyond two years due to the volatility in the market. I projected the losses to five years, at the request of BMI's attorney, to illustrate the impact of the 25 percent discount rate as compared to Dr. Seligman's lower rate.

Preparation of Opinion and Report

In preparing my report I created an initial draft, which I shared with BMI attorneys. We discussed minor alterations in my report. I made those changes and submitted a final report. I do not have a specific recollection of the differences in the two drafts. I do remember that when I met with the attorney for BMI we had an electronic version of my report, and we jointly made revisions in the report. I do not believe that BMI's attorney changed the meaning of any of my opinions or findings. BMI's attorney simply made suggestions to make my report more readable.

I do not have a copy of my original draft, either in hard copy or in electronic form. My preparation of the report, and my preparation for the deposition, probably took a total of fifteen hours. I charged BMI my usual consultation fee of $250 per hour, plus expenses, for research and preparation and $450 per hour, plus expenses, for testimony. I just keep hours spent on a project.

Maybe I should, but I don't keep specifics on how I spend each minute. I don't have any specific records of how much of that fifteen hours involved meeting with BMI's attorney, but I would speculate that I have met with them face-to-face for a total of three hours in preparing for my deposition and in preparing my report. I have no idea why BMI selected me. As I stated in my résumé, I have consulted with parties claiming personal injuries approximately seventeen times from YR-23 to the present. I've consulted with parties being sued for personal injury approximately two times since YR-23. Calculating economic damages for individuals and calculating economic damages for businesses involve the same type of economic analysis and the same methodology.

I do not feel that since my retirement the information in the industry has left me behind. Although I enjoy my leisure time more now, I do tend to keep up on the economic industry.

Knowledge of Seligman

In my experience, Dr. Seligman is a fine and respected young economist. However, Dr. Seligman has forgotten the lessons that we learned from the Great Depression. Dr. Seligman's inexperience in the economic academic world limits her understanding of the effect of the general economic market on specific industry markets. In my view, Dr. Seligman's career has been marked by mainly forensic experience with very little academic experience. I am not jealous of Dr. Seligman's success in the forensic world. I always relied on the academic world of the university for most of my income. The bulk of Dr. Seligman's income is from forensic consultations. I do not consider her to have the necessary academic background for this type of project.

I do not believe that Dr. Seligman's work in the computer industry early in her career gives any better insight for this case. That type of experience can be too narrow and limited. Although Dr. Seligman has some experience within an analogous computer market, my academic background gives me a broader perspective. Dr. Seligman spends a lot of time in conference rooms for depositions and in courtrooms for trial testimony. In my extensive academic career, I have spent more time examining broader economic trends.

In my opinion, Dr. Seligman did not consider adequately the impact of the start-up nature of Minicom and the highly volatile nature of the computer industry markets. Perhaps this is due to the fact that Dr. Seligman has forgotten the impact of the Great Depression and the severe impact of an economic slowdown on various markets. In addition, Dr. Seligman did not take into account Minicom's failure to mitigate their damages by seeking an alternative source for the computer chips sooner. In my opinion, Minicom just waited too long, thus aggravating their economic loss. Dr. Seligman puts too much stock in the veracity of data on the HWC market and the track record of Minicom.

Interview Preparation

Q: Describe for us how you prepared for this interview.

A: I probably spent two hours with the BMI attorneys preparing for my deposition. We discussed the questions that Minicom's attorneys might ask.

Q: What documents did the BMI attorneys provide you?

A: They gave me two new trade journal articles to read on the new computer markets. Those articles were not helpful, and I did not rely on them for my opinions.

Q: What did they tell you as to why they were giving you these two journals?

A: We discussed my lack of experience in the technology markets.

Q: What effect does your inexperience in technology markets have on your ability to give an opinion in this case?

A: Very little effect. I still feel confident that traditional economic principles apply to these new markets.

Q: What concerns do you have about the conduct of any of the BMI people in this case?

A: None, really. My only concern in the facts is that I get the impression that Chris Kay was not always "minding the store" when the order got lost, but it had no effect on the outcome of the lost shipment.

LAWRENCE D. SINGELL

PERSONAL DATA

Home Address
9144 Arvada
Nita City, Nita 80303
Telephone: (303) 394-9555

Date and Place of Birth
March 9, YR-65
Milwaukee, Wisconsin

EDUCATIONAL RECORD

BA, Economics, Beloit College, YR-42; MA, Economics, Nita State University, YR-40; PhD, Economics, Nita University, YR-37

PROFESSIONAL EXPERIENCE

Current Position

Nita University Professor of Economics (Emeritus)	September YR-1 to Present

Past Positions

Nita University, Professor of Economics	September YR-5 to August YR-1
Nita University, Professor of Economics & Chair of Department	June YR-20 to August YR-5
University of Pennsylvania, S. J. Small Chair in Economics (Visiting Professor)	Spring YR-20
University of Melbourne, Australia, Visiting Professor	Fall YR-21
University of Glasgow, Scotland, Visiting Professor (Adam Smith Chair)	Fall YR-22 and Spring YR-21
Nita University, Associate Professor	Fall YR-27 to Spring YR-22
Nita University, Assistant Professor	Fall YR-33 to Spring YR-27
Beloit College, Professor of Economics	Fall YR-37 to Spring YR-33

Teaching positions at Nita University, University of Pennsylvania, and University of Glasgow have involved teaching Human Factor Resources, Urban Economics, and Micro and Macro Theory. Received several distinguished teaching awards, including the Distinguished Teaching Award from the Student Alumni Association (SOAR) at Nita University and the Dorn Peterson Teaching Excellence Award in the Department of Economics, Beloit College.

OTHER PROFESSIONAL EXPERIENCE

Lecture in the American Economic Association's Visiting Scientists Program in Economics.
Director of Graduate Studies, Department of Economics, Nita University, YR-17 to YR-15.
Dean's Budget Advisory Committee, (several terms), Nita University.
Research Associate on a Milwaukee Area Economic Base Study, Beloit College, Summer YR-34.
Research Associate, Committee on Urban Economics, Resources for the Future, Washington, DC, in residence, Summer YR-20.
Economic Consultant, Department of Development, State of Nita, YR-19 to YR-17.

Economic Consultant, National Institute of Education, Department of Education, Department of Health, Education and Welfare, YR-25 to Y -23.

Served on the review or editorial board of the American Economic Review, Social Science Quarterly, Annals of Economics, Southern Economic Journal, Journal of Socio-Economics, and Samualson Journal of Macro-Economics.

PUBLICATIONS

Articles

"Some Private and Social Aspects of the Labor Mobility of Young Workers," *Quarterly Review of Economics*, vol. 9, no. 1 (Spring YR-30), pp. 19–29.

"An Examination of the Empirical Relationship between Unemployment and Juvenile Delinquency," *The Scotland Journal of Economics and Sociology*, vol. 16, no. 4 (YR -30), pp. 377–387.

"Barriers to Earning Income," *Quarterly Review of Economics*, vol. 12, no. 2 (Summer YR-29), pp. 35–44.

"The Simple Analytics of Hard-Core Unemployment," (with Edward Baker), *Southern Economic Journal*, vol. 7, no. 1 (April YR-29), pp. 51–60.

"A Note on the Use of Simulation Games in Interdisciplinary Graduate Education," *The Journal of Education*, vol. 2, no. 1 (Fall YR-26), pp. 61–63.

"Barriers to Business Profitability," *The Journal of Economics*, vol. 5, no. 2 (Winter YR-26), pp. 61–65.

"Variables of Doing Business on Business Development," *Northern Economic Journal* (January YR-25), pp. 63–41.

"An Empirical Analysis of the Discount Rate in Determining Profitability," *Journal of Economics*, no. 2 (YR-24), pp. 119–129.

"The Effects of Growth Management on the Housing Market: A Review of Theoretical and Empirical Evidence," *Journal of Urban Affairs*, vol. 9, no. 1 (Winter YR-24), pp. 63–78.

"Scottish Business Practices in the World Economy," *Scottish Journal of Economics and Sociology*, vol. 48, no. 4 (October YR-22), pp. 457–471.

"Salary Compression: An Empirical Evaluation of the Narrowing Gap between New Entrants and Senior Employees," *Journal of Socio-Economics*, vol. 21, no. 3 (YR-20), pp 1–21.

"Job Satisfaction, Salaries, and Unions: The Determination of University Faculty Compensation" (with Jane Lillydahl), *Economics of Education Review*, (forthcoming YR-15) vol. 12, no. 3.

"Will Changing Times Change the Allocation of Faculty Time in Research Universities?" (with Jane Lillydahl), *Journal of Human Resources*, vol. 31, no. 2 (Spring YR-12).

"Consumerism," *Consumer Economics Journal*, New York: Grolier, Inc. (YR-12), pp. 26–36.

"Investment in Education and Ghetto Poverty," *Social Economic Science Quarterly* (June YR-11), pp. 122–128.

"Planning an Incentive Model to Improve Efficiency in Education," *Social Economic Science Quarterly* (June YR-9), pp. 122–128.

MONOGRAPHS AND BOOKS

Business Economics and the Industrial Revolution, Wiley & Sons Press, New York, YR-33. Basic Economics in America, Samualson Press, New York, YR-27.

Basic Economics in America, Second Edition, Samualson Press, New York, YR-20.

The Problem of Obtaining and Using Resources in Education: Some Proposed Programs for Purposive Change (with several other authors), National Institute of Education, Department of Health, Education and Welfare (December YR-10), pp. 1–115 and statistical appendix.

An Analysis of Taxing and Expenditure Policies in the City of Nita with Special Reference to Optimal City Size, The Nita Area Growth Study Commission (August YR-9), pp. 1–149.

Market Failure and Government Failure: Some Lessons for Public Policy and the Quality of Life, Socialist Center for the Study of Social Values, Nita University, YR-7.

PAPERS PRESENTED AT PROFESSIONAL MEETINGS

American Economic Association; Pacific Economic Association; Midwest Economic Association Meetings; Western Economic Association Meetings; Michigan Economic Society; Southern Regional Science Association; Appalachian Mountain Social Science Association Meetings; Eastern Social Science Association; Urban Affairs Association

MEMBERSHIPS IN PROFESSIONAL ASSOCIATIONS

American Economic Association; Nita State Economics Association; City of Nita Economics Study Group

RESEARCH INTERESTS

Human Resource Problems Relating to the Urban Environment

TEACHING INTERESTS

Human Resources; Urban Economics; Intermediate Economic Theory; Introductory Economics

LEGAL CONSULTATIONS

Trial Testimony on projected economic loss for injured plaintiffs (approximately seventeen times) YR-23 to Present

Trial Testimony on projected economic loss for defense (approximately two times) YR-23 to Present

Trial Testimony for Nita Center for Urban Renewal (6 times) in zoning commission hearings and one class action YR-24 to Present

Approximately 35 Depositions in litigation (80 percent on behalf of damaged party) YR-23 to Present

RULE 26 DISCLOSURES

Compensation
Preparation and Research $250.00 per hour, plus expenses
Deposition and Trial Testimony $450.00 per hour, plus expenses

Testimony in Last Four Years
Shirley Sanders v. St. Mary's Hospital—Nita District Court—Health Care Negligence Wrongful Death—June YR-2 Deposition and July YR-1 Trial Testimony (Retained by Defendant Hospital)
Peter Papas v. Pharmu Pharmaceuticals—Federal District Court (E.D. Pa.)—Product Liability Diet Pill Wrongful Death—April YR-2 Deposition (Retained by Plaintiff)

Silvia Stephens v. Stanley Schmidt—Nita District Court—Automobile Collision—June YR-3 Deposition (Retained by Plaintiff)

Louise Natali v. Walstore Super Center—Federal District Court (D. Colo.)—Business Losses Due to Lease Breach—September YR-4 Deposition and April YR-3 Trial (Retained by Plaintiff)

EXPERT REPORT OF DR. SELIGMAN

AN EVALUATION OF THE ECONOMIC LOSS TO MINICOM INC. FROM FAILURE OF BMI TO DELIVER ON CONTRACT

The purpose of this report is to evaluate, based on reasonable economic probabilities, the economic loss to Minicom Inc. from the alleged failure of Business Machines Incorporated (BMI) to deliver 100 gross of integrated chip platforms in a manner consistent with a contract between these two firms. The Court ordered Minicom to disclose expert opinions before BMI due to the fact that Minicom claims substantial losses in their counterclaim. As a factual predicate for this evaluation, I have received from defendant's counsel and reviewed the pleadings; the exhibits marked as Exhibits 1–42; and the depositions of Lubell, Milstein, Kay, and Young. Minicom is in the business of manufacturing, selling, and distributing computers known in the trade as handheld wearable computers (HWC). The market for HWCs is growing rapidly, and Minicom was establishing a reputation as the leading firm in this field. BMI, a non-competitor in the HWC field, produced and supplied the integrated chip platforms that Minicom used in its production. Although there were other suppliers for integrated chip platforms, Minicom had previously relied on BMI to supply these parts, and in the dispute under evaluation in this report, had entered into a virtually identical contract to deliver 100 gross of integrated chip platforms.

These integrated chip platforms were lost in shipment, and after a considerable delay caused by BMI, Minicom was forced to order these parts from an alternative supplier. As a result, Minicom:

1) had to pay $50,000 more for these parts in order to obtain the delivery as quickly as possible;

2) lost sales, and the related profits on said sales, from the date of the expected delivery until July 3, YR-0, the date of trial in this matter; and

3) lost one of their major buyers of their HWC product.

This firm, Nieman Marcus, it is alleged, cancelled their order and has discontinued doing business with Minicom Inc. because of Minicom's failure to deliver product in a timely manner. The purpose of this report is to evaluate, based on reasonable economic probabilities, the lost profits and increased cost, which in effect reduces profits, incurred by Minicom from this failure to supply these integrated chips in a timely manner. For purposes of this evaluation, it is assumed that Minicom's allegations of BMI's contract failure are valid. This economic loss is evaluated in two time periods:

1) from the date of this failure to deliver to the trial date on July 3, YR-0; and

2) lost profits into the future.

The past loss in profits and the increased costs may be summarized as follows:

Year	Description of Loss	Value of Loss
YR-1	Lost Profits: 20,000 unit order at $20 per unit contribution	$400,000
YR-1	Increased cost of 100 gross ICP-73s	$ 50,000
TOTAL PAST LOST		$450,000

Minicom alleges that just prior to trial they lost one of the major buyers of their HWC products as a result of this delay in parts delivery. Accepting this allegation as valid makes it reasonably likely that losses will continue into the future. Indeed, the highly competitive nature of this market makes continued customer satisfaction a vital element in maintaining market share. Indeed, the loss of an order of 20,000 HWC per year could continue indefinitely into the future unless Minicom can, through some special effort and expenditure of resources, reestablish its reputation for timely delivery. From an economic point of view, the loss of this order has two components, which together represent the loss in profits to Minicom as follows:

1) The direct loss in profits from these 20,000 units. Accounting records for the firm demonstrate that at the 100,000 units per year output rate, which Minicom had at the time of the alleged contract failure, the firm's profit per unit was $20. Hence, this loss of sales of 20,000 units results in a direct profit loss of $400,000 per year.

2) A further indirect loss in profits results because at a lower scale of operation, unit production costs are higher. In short, this occurs because overhead costs must be spread over a smaller volume of output. The firm's accounting records show that unit costs are $3 per unit higher with output and sales of 80,000 as compared with 100,000. Hence, the profits on each continuing unit of output are reduced by $3 per unit. Thus, this indirect loss in profits is $240,000 per year.

In what follows, these future losses of profit are evaluated for two, five, and ten years into the future. This represents the most probable time frame in which these losses will continue. It should be noted that this evaluation does not consider expenditures that Minicom might have to make to restore its image as a producer with a reputation for timely and reliable delivery.

Future losses in profits are reduced to a present value using a discount rate, which incorporates the level of risk for start-up firms in American industry. The discount rate used is 8.5 percent, the long-run average rate of interest on corporate securities. Thus, this rate of 8.5 percent represents the rate that individuals engaged in arms-length transactions must receive to provide capital to such business. Discounting yields a sum of money that must be provided at the date of trial to place Minicom in the same position in terms of the economic value of the enterprise. In short, it just compensates Minicom in present value dollars for the lost profits that result from the loss in future sales.

Based upon the above, the future losses may be summarized as follows:

Future Loss in Profits to Minicom Inc.					
	Direct Loss of Profits of 20,000 Units		Indirect Loss from Increased Costs of Smaller Scale		
Duration of Loss in Years	Value of Loss	Present Value	Value of Loss	Present Value	Total Present Value of Loss
2	$800,000	$708,400	$480,000	$425,100	$1,133,500
5	$2,000,000	$1,576,300	$1,200,000	$945,800	$2,522,100
10	$4,000,000	$2,624,500	$2,400,000	$1,574,700	$4,199,200

Thus, in my opinion, based upon reasonable economic probabilities, the present value of the past and future loss in profits to Minicom is between $1,583,500 and $4,749,200. The lower evaluation of the loss assumes that Minicom will be able to reestablish its reputation for timely delivery and a foothold in the more sophisticated HWC market in only two years, while the higher range in the loss evaluation assumes this will take ten years. There is some probability that they may never be able to completely restore their reputation.

In my judgment, the assumptions made in evaluating this loss are conservative and some elements of possible loss may be overlooked. For example, there could be other future losses of orders that result from this delay in parts delivery and therefore result in a reduction of production and reduced profits. Since discovery is still continuing in this matter, the opinion expressed here must be taken as preliminary. I would be willing to review additional information that may be forthcoming in this discovery and to present my final opinion of the loss for the court's consideration.

Barbara Seligman
Center for Economic Studies Nita University

June 30, YR-1

BBS/bs

INTERVIEW WITH DR. SELIGMAN

OCTOBER 20, YR-1

DR. SELIGMAN gave the following answers in an interview with the attorneys.

Dr. Seligman began her interview by corroborating the information on her résumé regarding qualifications as well as her Rule 26 disclosures regarding testimony within the last four years and publications within the past ten years. She then stated that she stood by the opinion contained in her report. In addition, Dr. Seligman provided the following information:

Q: What effect does the discount rate used by an economist have on the present value of the economist's lost profits estimate?

A: They are inversely proportional. The lower the discount rate the economist chooses, the higher the present value of the economist's estimate of lost profits. The higher the discount rate chosen, the lower the present value of the lost profits estimate.

Q: What discount rate did you apply to your lost profits estimate to determine its present value?

A: 8.5 percent.

Q: To what estimate of lost profits did you apply this 8.5 percent discount rate?

A: The estimated future lost profits of Minicom regarding the Neiman Marcus account and related accounts in the sale of the handheld wearable computers (HWC).

Q: How did you determine that there was an agreement between Neiman Marcus and Minicom for the purchase of HWC products?

A: I spoke with Dr. Elliot Milstein, who made the agreement, and I was shown an exchange of e-mail that confirmed the agreement. [*Assume that this e-mail has been produced and it supports the conclusion that there was a contract between Neiman Marcus and Minicom for the purchase of 5,000 HWC units in YR-1 and an expected, but not yet formalized, additional order for 15,000 units in the future.*] In addition, Dr. Milstein confirmed that assuming satisfaction with the quality of the HWC product, Neiman Marcus predicted purchases in the range of 20,000 units per year for future years.

Q: Did you actually see a written agreement in which Neiman Marcus said it would buy anything more than the initial 5,000 units?

A: Dr. Milstein told me that after discussions there was an agreement in principle, but that the sales never happened because when Minicom never got the parts from BMI, Minicom could not make timely delivery of the Neiman Marcus order.

Q: You didn't confirm that alleged "agreement in principle" with anyone, did you?

A: No, of course not. I had no access to the people at Neiman Marcus. I should add that no economist in my position would speak with anyone other than the party that retained her in verifying the facts of the underlying transaction. I followed precisely the methods utilized for obtaining such information used by all economists in my field and assumed the accuracy of what Mr. Milstein told me and what he testified to in his deposition.

Q: On what do you base your assertion that the late delivery of ICPs caused Minicom's failure to make timely delivery of the HWC product to Neiman Marcus?

A: Again, I relied on conversation with Dr. Milstein, his deposition, and conversation with his Vice President for Production, Mr. Bentley, as would any economist. According to Mr. Bentley, the manufacturing process of the HWCs required the availability of ICPs throughout the process, not just at one juncture. When the ICPs were late, production had to stop. In addition, the replacement part was so configured as to require some design modifications to the HWC produced for Neiman Marcus. I assumed that he was accurate in that regard.

Q: What did you assume regarding whether Minicom acted promptly in replacing the ICP shipment that was lost by NPS?

A: I assumed they did. According to correspondence I reviewed and the depositions of Dr. Milstein and Mr. Kay, Dr. Milstein was in consultation with Mr. Kay at BMI, and Mr. Kay did not finally refuse to replace the lost shipment without payment until after March 1, YR-1. At that point it was too late to fulfill the Neiman Marcus order, and the customer was lost.

Q: Again, the information you relied on came from Minicom officers and employees?

A: Yes, as well as a document I reviewed—I believe a phone log on the subject.

Q: In your estimate of losses, you projected losses out for periods of two, five, and ten years?

A: That's right.

Q: And it was to those estimates of losses that you applied the 8.5 percent discount rate you told us about?

A: That's correct.

Q: What was your basis for selecting an 8.5 percent discount rate?

A: I chose the 8.5 percent discount rate due to the long-term stability in the market of the entire computer industry. Computers, especially small, light, and mobile computers, have become the standard communication and data collection tool of every industry. The HWC product produced by Minicom and the anticipated upgraded models of the future would have situated them well for a substantial share of the market, thereby providing the company with great stability.

Q: So you believe that the future earnings of a more stable company should be discounted less than those of a less stable company, all other things being equal?

A: Yes.

Q: In other words, you would use a lower discount rate for the more stable company than you would for the less stable company?

A: Exactly.

Q: And would the converse also be true, that for an unstable company you would use a higher discount rate than for a stable company, again, all other things being equal?

A: As a general matter, I agree with that proposition.

Q: You have also assumed that Minicom would improve the technology of its HWC products over time, is that correct?

A: Yes, that was Dr. Milstein's plan and is the obvious plan for any business in that industry. Improvements and new products are the way that profitability is maintained and increased. All you have to do is look at the Apple iPod products to understand that fact. Unfortunately, the problem with Neiman Marcus caused Minicom to lose its foothold in that industry.

Q: But of course, Minicom could gain a new foothold with another retailer, right?

A: That would be speculation for me to agree with that statement.

Q: I want to go back to your selection of the 8.5 percent discount rate for your estimate in this case. What was the method you used to select that rate?

A: In researching the appropriate discount rate in this case, I used standard economic research principles.

Q: What do you mean by standard economic research principles?

A: I looked at the sources of information economists normally look at and rely on when determining the proper discount rate to utilize—what a competent and well-informed economist would do in the same situation.

Q: What sources did you consult?

A: I first looked at the United States Department of Labor and Department of Commerce statistics to determine the general economic behavior of the industry market.

Q: Why did you do that?

A: The statistics provided by these governmental entities tend to be the most reliable and objective sources for this sort of information.

Q: What did those sources suggest regarding the discount rate in this case?

A: Although there was no information regarding the HWC market in particular, there was information about the manufacture and sale of small electronic consumer products that are similar to the HWC that gave me good insight into the economy of the industry in question. I was able to find analogous markets for laptop computers, Blackberries, and cell phones, all of which provide similar functions to the HWC. This led me to conclude that a discount rate of 8.5 percent, which approximates the historic long-term borrowing rate of corporations in that market, would be appropriate.

Q: But isn't there a distinction between established companies like Apple, IBM, and Motorola, and a start-up like Minicom?

A: If Minicom was fairly categorized as a start-up company, perhaps, but I do not accept that characterization. While it is true that they are a newer company without a long track record, I would not characterize Minicom as a mere start-up company. Given the nature of the product (the HWC), the reputation of its designer, Dr. Milstein, and the quality of his management team, most of whom came from very successful careers with well-established firms, as well as the burgeoning current status and promising future of the electronics information industry, I determined that Minicom would likely have received the general historic corporate rate as a long-term borrower, and as such the 8.5 percent discount rate was reasonable and appropriate.

Q: Were there other sources you consulted in selecting the 8.5 percent discount rate?

A: Yes, I also researched data in trade publications and trade databases concerning the HWC market and found additional data that was generally supportive of the 8.5 percent discount rate. This trade data is almost as reliable as the government source I told you about, especially in my personal experience as an economist in the computer industry.

Q: Are you referring to your experience at StorageDataTek as the Chief Operating Officer?

A: Yes, while we did not produce HWC products (they did not exist at that time), we were in the business of marketing, selling, and distributing computer storage memory parts, which were state of the art at the time.

Q: And that experience was in YR-14 through YR-12?

A: Yes, but I have always kept up with the industry and its growth.

Q: How would this experience be of assistance to you in this case?

A: Because of my direct industry experience, I am able to judge which trade publications and database information can be relied on and which information is unreliable due to competitive "puffing" and other data bias. Absent experience in the industry, an economist would not know on which information he or she could safely rely.

Q: What information that you found in trade publications and industry databases did you use in deciding that you should use an 8.5 percent discount rate?

A: That the HWC market was a promising and growing one—there was a specific article in one of the noted trade publications, *Computer World,* in YR-2 that foreshadowed the expected availability of the Minicom HWC product that was very flattering to Mr. Milstein and his design capabilities, noting his success at i-Gloo.

Q: Did you contact *Computer World* to find out what led to the publication of that article?

A: No.

Q: Was there anything else from trade publications and industry databases you relied on in deciding to use an 8.5 percent discount rate?

A: I am sure there was, but I can't remember it now.

Q: Did you have any other sources for information on which you relied in choosing an 8.5 percent discount rate to use in this case?

A: Next in the standard economic analysis is to analogize the HWC market to the market for similar products; this is commonly done by virtually all economists when performing an analysis such as this.

Q: And how did that inform your choice of a discount rate in this case?

A: I found the level of technological development resulting in periodic upgrading for the emerging HWC market to be similar in the analogous markets involving laptops, Blackberries and similar devices, and cell phones. That data increased my confidence that I had correctly determined 8.5 percent to be the appropriate discount rate.

Q: Did you do anything else in determining the discount rate to use here?

A: Just to be sure, I followed the common practice of consulting with an expert in the industry.

Q: Just one?

A: Yes.

Q: Who did you consult?

A: The budget for this engagement did not allow for hiring an independent consultant, so I did what is frequently done in analyses of this sort and confirmed my understanding of the technical aspects of the market with an insider; here, Dr. Milstein.

Q: Didn't Dr. Milstein's obvious financial interest in the outcome of the case cause you some concern?

A: Not really, because all I was asking him about were my conclusions about the computer industry, and with more particularity, the HWC market. He did not know why I was asking the questions, and he is not an economist who deals with discount rates on a regular basis. After all, he had invested a significant amount of money in that market, so it was in his interest to accurately evaluate that market. When he confirmed all that I had found from independent sources, I was able to use his confirmation to strengthen my opinion as to the propriety of the 8.5 percent discount rate. This was obviously a growing and dynamic market in which Minicom was involved, and Minicom had been well-situated in that market before this problem with BMI.

Q: Did you do anything else before finally choosing the 8.5 percent discount rate for use in this case?

A: As best I can remember it, that's it.

A: Did you consider that Minicom had never had a positive cash flow up to and including the time in question in this lawsuit?

A: I did, but they would have had a positive cash flow but for the problem with BMI in YR-1. I couldn't reasonably increase the discount rate based on BMI's actions and inactions. In addition, once a company breaks through in an emerging market, they become attractive risks for long-term investment—all of which is consistent with the discount rate I chose.

Q: Why did you assume that to the extent that the loss of the Neiman Marcus account had an effect on lost profits to Minicom, the effect would continue for up to ten years?

A: Minicom, after the events of YR-1, would have to overcome a reputation for untimely delivery. That is the sort of reputation that might have effects on profitability lasting well beyond ten years.

Q: By the way, have you ever utilized a discount rate of 8.5 percent in any of your previous engagements to calculate estimated lost profits for a corporation?

A: Yes, I have used that rate in matters involving established corporate entities, as I am sure you have found in reviewing my previous testimony.

Q: In fact, weren't all of the companies you were engaged by in the past considered "blue chip" companies?

A: That's right.

Q: Certainly you don't consider Minicom to be a "blue chip" company, do you?

A: I consider Minicom to be a special case—a special company—with a special product—in a special industry. The computer industry welcomes and embraces such companies in a way that fast tracks them to "blue chip" status, a recognition that the company is a great investment. No sector of the economy is as fast-moving and fast-growing as the electronic information industry in which Mini-com was on its way to becoming a rising star.

Q: Couldn't Minicom use its special status and special product to overcome any potential damage to profitability in less time than you have calculated, perhaps even less than two years?

A: Perhaps, but they would need some luck, and I can't do an analysis on the assumption that a company will be lucky.

Barbara Seligman

2244 Candalera Place   DOB August 12, YR-42
Nita City, Nita 80303
Telephone: (303) 421-8935

EDUCATION

BA, Business Administration, Indiana University, YR-21; MBA, Indiana University, YR-20; PhD, Economics, Nita University, YR-17

EXPERIENCE

Center for Economic Studies, President   YR-12 to Present

> Economic consulting firm, specializing in business planning, business operations, earnings forecasting, and revenue projection for business plans/business proposals, litigation support, and forensic services.

StorageDataTek, Chief Operating Officer   YR-14 to YR-12

> Responsible for all marketing, sales, and distribution operations for worldwide sales and distribution of computer memory storage component parts.

StorageDataTek, Management Trainee and Assistant to COO   YR-17 to YR-14

> Responsible for assisting COO with all marketing, sales, and distribution operations for worldwide sales and distribution of computer memory storage component parts.

PUBLICATIONS

"Product Distribution Strategies for the Emerging Global Economy," *Quarterly Review of Economics*, vol. 26, no. 2 (Spring YR-19) (PhD Dissertation Nita University, faculty sponsor, L. Singell, YR-17).

MEMBERSHIPS

American Economic Association; Nita Economic Association; International Society of Forensic Economists.

EXPERT TESTIMONY

Qualified as expert in economic projection of profits, losses, and damages in state and federal courts for Nita and twenty-four other states.

Current Consultation Scale

> Research, investigation, and report writing—$350.00 per hour, plus expenses.

> Deposition testimony—$700 per hour, plus expenses (time calculated portal to portal).

> Trial/Arbitration Testimony—$1,250 per hour, plus expenses (time calculated portal to portal).

Clients and References

> Nita National Bank; Nita Liability Insurance Company; Nita Board of Adjustment; Microsoft; WorldCom, Inc.; Nike International; Nita Dumb Friends League

RULE 26 DISCLOSURES OF PAST TESTIMONY

Leveno Computers v. Gustafson—Federal District Court (S.D. Fla.)—Patent Infringement—June YR-1 Deposition (Retained by Plaintiff Leveno)

Leveno Computers v. Pharmu Pharmaceuticals—Federal District Court (E.D. Pa.)—Breach of Contract—March YR-1 Deposition (Retained by Plaintiff Leveno)

Schlotsky v. Idol Time Software—Federal District Court (E.D. Va.)—Breach of Contract—December YR-2 Deposition and April YR-1 Trial (Retained by Defendant Idol Time)

StorageDataTek v. MicroSpam—Federal District Court (N.D. Ca.)—Breach of Contract—October YR-2 Deposition and May YR-1 Trial Testimony (Retained by Plaintiff StorageDataTek)

Laveno Computers v. MicroSpam—Federal District Court (N.D. Ca.)—Breach of Contract—June YR-2 Deposition and June YR-1 Trial Testimony (Retained by Plaintiff Leveno)

State of Colorado v. StorageDataTek—Federal District Court (D. Colo.)—Antitrust Investigation—October YR-3 Deposition and March YR-1 Trial Testimony (Retained by Defendant StorageDataTek)

StorageDataTek v. Treasure Fields—Federal District Court (N.D. Ca.)—Breach of Contract—July YR-3 Deposition and January YR-1 Trial Testimony (Retained by Plaintiff StorageDataTek)

Peterson v. Winslow—Nita District Court (Nita)—Breach of Lease—January YR-3 Deposition and October YR-2 Trial Testimony (Retained by Plaintiff Peterson)

State of Nita v. Microspam—Nita Federal District Court—Antitrust—February YR-3 Deposition and August YR-2 Trial (Retained by State of Nita)

Lasko v. Longtime LLC—Nita District Court (Nita)—Breach of Contract—August YR-3 Deposition and June YR-2 Trial (Retained by Defendant Longtime LLC)

Grossman v. Manning—Federal District Court (S.D. Fla.)—Patent Infringement—May YR-2 Deposition (Retained by Plaintiff Grossman)

In Re: Grossman—Federal District Court and Bankruptcy Court (S.D. Fla.)—Bankruptcy Proceedings—March YR-4 Deposition, July YR-4 Deposition, September YR-3 Trustee Hearing, and January YR-3 Meeting of Creditors (Retained by Debtor Grossman)

Plastiko v. Scamway LLC—Nita District Court (Nita)—Breach of Contract—July YR-4 Deposition and January YR-3 Trial Testimony (Retained by Plaintiff Plastiko)

State of Nita v. FlashCube Platforms LLC—Nita Federal District Court—Antitrust—February YR-4 Deposition and August YR-3 Trial (Retained by State of Nita)

StorageDataTek v. Microspam—Federal District Court (N.D. Ca.)—Breach of Contract—July YR-5 Deposition and January YR-4 Trial Testimony (Retained by Plaintiff StorageDataTek)

Torres v. Lansing—Nita District Court—Breach of Contract—May YR-4 Deposition (Retained by Defendant Lansing)

Lostway, Inc. v. Stansfield—Nita District Court—Breach of Lease—March YR-5 Deposition and February YR-4 Trial (Retained by Defendant Stansfield)

StorageDataTek v. Classman—Nita District Court—Breach of Contract—January YR-5 Deposition and February YR-4 Trial Testimony (Retained by Plaintiff StorageDataTek)

StorageDataTek v. Wall—Nita District Court—Breach of Contract—April YR-4 Deposition (Retained by Plaintiff StorageDataTek)

State of Nita v. BMI, Inc.—Nita Federal District Court—Antitrust—February YR-6 Deposition and January YR-5 Trial (Retained by State of Nita)

MATERIALS AVAILABLE
ONLY TO THE PLAINTIFF'S LAW FIRM
(BMI'S COUNSEL)

STATEMENT OF CHRISTOPHER KAY

JULY 22, YR-1

My name is Christopher Kay, but I go by "Chris" both personally and professionally. I am thirty-four years old. I live at 11 Darby Road in Brookline, Massachusetts. I am married to my wife, Andrea, and we have two children: Chris Jr., age eight, and Lisa, age five. Andrea and I have been married for ten years, since YR-10.

I grew up in Westport, Connecticut, where I attended the public schools. After high school I went to Williams College and graduated cum laude with a degree in Economics in YR-11. Following graduation from Williams I took a financial analyst position with the World Venture Fund (WFD) on Wall Street. I had always thought that I would be more successful in a corporate setting and realized that to reach that goal in the market at the time, I needed an MBA degree. So, in YR-10, with Andrea supporting us by working as a nurse and some student loans, I enrolled in the MBA program at the University of North Carolina. I received my MBA magna cum laude from UNC in YR-8.

After graduating from UNC, I took a job as a management trainee with Business Machines Incorporated (BMI) in their Brookline office and have been employed there ever since. BMI is an international electronics firm and is in the business of manufacturing electronic equipment, including computers, as well as selling electronic parts to other companies. My current job is sales manager for Subdivision II of the Eastern Region of BMI, which is located in Brookline, Massachusetts. BMI divides its operations into five regions in the United States. Each region is divided into subdivisions. The Eastern Region has six subdivisions. My subdivision is the largest in the Eastern Region. We employ 105 people at the Brookline facility. We do not manufacture any of our products in Brookline. We are solely a sales and distribution facility and have a total of twenty-five warehouses on approximately twelve acres.

My job as the sales manager is to oversee the Brookline facility. The job involves direct supervision of a sales staff, which includes three assistant sales managers, six sales assistants, twelve deputy sales assistants, and a number of management trainees and support staff. My main responsibilities are to oversee supervision of existing accounts, find new accounts, sell products, and manage the distribution center. BMI's main business is sales of electronic parts used in manufacturing such products as computing devices, mobile devices, televisions, and civilian and military telecommunications equipment.

In YR-2, an emerging market for us was the handheld wearable computing device industry. These devices are generally known as HWCs. HWCs are used by most high-end mobile professionals and business types. These devices are a combination of a laptop computer, PDA (personal data assistant), camera and mobile phone, most of which also have GPS (global positioning system) capability and digital videography capabilities. BMI does not produce its own HWC, but we are a major supplier of component parts for such devices.

In the eight years I have been with BMI, I have been promoted from management trainee to deputy sales assistant in YR-7, to sales assistant in YR-6, to assistant sales manager in YR-5, and to sales manager in YR-3, all in Eastern Subdivision II. Compared to others who began with me as a management trainee, my promotion rate has been the fastest in our subdivision. I have every intention of remaining with BMI for my career. It is an excellent company with great benefits and a bright future. The next promotion for me would be to the regional level from the subdivision level. In fact, in January of YR-1, I was being considered for an opening as the sales manager for the Eastern Region that was expected to come open in June of that year due to a retirement.

That job would have been the first step to upper level management at BMI. It would have meant a substantial raise as well. My current salary is $140,000 per year, and the salary range for a regional sales manager is $165,000 to $195,000, with the possibility of bonuses ranging up to $30,000 per year.

I did not get that promotion. I can't say for sure why I was passed over, but this problem with Minicom may have had something to do with it. The woman who received the appointment, however, had been with BMI for five more years than me and was certainly qualified for the job. I am sure that I will be considered for other promotions in the future, especially after this gets cleared up.

At the time that we first did business with Minicom, I had been in my present position for about a year. Virginia Young has been my administrative assistant since YR-7, when I became a deputy sales assistant. While I was a management trainee and was working on a project, Virginia did some work for me out of the temporary administrative assistant pool. We got along very well, so when I was eligible for an administrative assistant I asked her to work for me full time, which was a promotion for her. We have been a good team ever since. Each time I was promoted I asked her to come along as my administrative assistant. It was my intention to bring her to the regional position if it had been offered to me. I don't know whether she would have accepted. It never came to that.

Virginia is married to one of my assistant sales managers, Dan Macon. They met each other at a holiday party at my house in YR-4, and they were married the next year. Virginia's job is to handle much of the administration associated with my position in addition to taking care of almost all my correspondence, scanning to digital filing, taking phone messages when I am out, and making and tracking my appointments. She takes the phone messages because it is company policy for all sales departments not to use voice mail—we want customers to actually talk to a real person every time they call. BMI maintains its records electronically. We no longer have traditional files. Although written communications are a big part of our business, everything we receive that we keep is scanned into our digital files, as are copies of paper documents that we send out to others, but want kept in our files.

Virginia's job duties include taking care of all of my correspondence, filing, making and keeping track of appointments, taking phone messages, opening e-mail, etc. In addition, Virginia takes care of more personal matters, including making tennis court and haircut appointments, reminding me of birthdays and other special events, as well as keeping my personal calendar. Doing those personal things for me is not part of her job description nor typical for a BMI assistant. She started doing those things on her own to help me be more efficient at my job.

Virginia is extremely well versed in the operation of our office. She routinely processes orders, and she is authorized, when I am not available, to sign routine correspondence like form thank you letters for orders. Virginia does have customer contact. The customers tell me that they really appreciate how well she treats them. She answers my phone and e-mails, and she often provides information to customers about pricing and availability of our products. She is not, however, authorized to enter into contracts on behalf of BMI. As between her and me, only I can do that.

The first time we made any contact with Minicom was in July of YR-2. I should preface this by saying that in preparing for my testimony I reviewed the Minicom file. By "Minicom file," I mean the digital file of all documents relating to Minicom as a client. This file is kept by Virginia on our server.

I know that I produced a copy of that electronic file to our lawyers to provide to you. I also reviewed all the stuff you lawyers call ESI, other electronically stored information that we had related to Minicom. I know we also gave that to our lawyers to give to you.

The first I heard of Minicom was when I ran one of my periodic Internet searches to learn more about new companies in our space who might be potential buyers of BMI's products. Minicom popped up as a new player in the HWC market and therefore a potential customer for our electronic parts, especially our integrated chip platforms (ICPs). ICPs are electronic parts on which are mounted several subparts. Each subpart has the electronic instructions for a common electronic device such as a computer, phone, or GPS. Right around the first of July of YR-2, we mailed a brochure and price lists for several of our products to them. One of those price lists was the one for ICPs. Exhibit 1 is a copy of the price list for ICPs that we mailed to Minicom.

The first time I spoke to anyone from Minicom was in early September of YR-2. I received a call from a Michael Lubell, who identified himself as the Vice President for Purchasing at Minicom. He told me that he was surveying the ICP manufacturers—I think he mentioned Exrox and Houston Instruments—and that he had a copy of our ICP price list and that he was interested in purchasing 100 gross of ICPs. After some conversation about the technical requirements for the ICP they designed into their HWC, we identified the ICP-73 as the platform that suited their needs. Yes, Lubell was well versed in the technical end of his needs and therefore the identification process was very easily accomplished. He did not, however, seem as fluent in the business end of the transaction.

In that phone call, I confirmed for Mr. Lubell that our price was $5,000 per gross as stated on the price list. He then told me that he would like to place the order with me. I explained to Mr. Lubell that it was BMI's policy not to accept phone or e-mail orders and that we would need for him to either fax or mail his order to us. We still insist on hard-copy orders because of the high cost and technical nature of our products, and we want to be sure that the customer gets exactly what the customer wants. That requirement, which is well within the norm in our industry, seemed to surprise him. I think that he tried to place his order over the phone, even after our conversation about the need for a hard copy order. I did not tell him this, but we do make an exception to our fax and mail order only policy for long-term customers in emergency situations. In an emergency situation, I am the only person in my subdivision authorized to accept an e-mail order or a pre-written confirmation telephone order. I have done this only twice since I have been the sales manager for this subdivision. In both cases the customer had been with us for over five years and averaged approximately seven to ten orders per year, so the way we did business with them was well settled.

In my conversation with Lubell, we also talked about his need for shipment in ten days, that National Parcel Service (NPS) was our preferred shipper and acceptable to them, and confirmed our payment conditions that appear on our price list, providing 2 percent discount for payment within thirty days; billing price for payment within sixty days; and 1.5 percent finance charge for each thirty-day period, or part thereof, for payments after sixty days of billing. Lubell also said that he wanted us to declare excess valuation or otherwise provide insurance for the shipment to protect Minicom in case the shipment was lost by the shipper or damaged in any way after it left our hands. Excess valuation means that we were to tell the shipper that the goods were worth more than the minimum coverage the shipper itself provided on all shipments. Such a request is unusual in our industry as most companies have "blanket" risk of loss policies that cover all incoming shipments, but we, of course, followed his directions to the order. The shipment insurance request, although unusual, is sometimes made in the case of start-up companies that are watching their costs very closely. After the failed attempt at a phone order, Mr. Lubell put all of these terms in the order that we received by both fax and mail, although either one of them would have been sufficient. Exhibit 3A is the fax cover sheet, 3B is the fax, and 3C is the letter. The fax was received the day of our conversation, and the letter several days later.

As usual, I had Virginia process the order, which she did by sending a work order to Warehouse 22, which handles ICPs (Exhibit 4). The order was shipped with a declaration of excess valuation via NPS (Exhibit 5). Once shipment was made, I sent a thank-you note (Exhibit 6) (which is a form letter), together with an invoice (Exhibit 7) to Minicom. The purpose of the letter and invoice is two-fold as is clear from the letter—to say thanks and to be sure that we had shipped out the right goods on the right terms. It was my hope that Minicom would become a long-term customer for us. Apparently the parts were in good order, because we received payment within thirty days, and per our policy, Minicom got the 2 percent discount on the order (see Exhibits 8 and 9).

In the hopes of nurturing our business relationship with Minicom, I decided to invite a representative to our Eastern Regional Exposition of Computer-Related Products in Hilton Head, South Carolina, in December of YR-2. The exposition is an event that allows us to wine and dine potential as well as long-time customers. I had enough in my marketing budget to invite thirty of my customers to this event. Little or no business is actually transacted during Expo, but good business relationships are fostered, which often lead to new or increased sales. After checking around, I determined that Minicom was a small company that was the brainchild of its president and CEO, Elliot Milstein, so I invited him instead of Lubell, whose position at Minicom was the rough equivalent of a mid-level buyer at BMI.

I spoke with Mr. Milstein sometime in November of YR-2, and he said he was interested in attending, especially after I told him that we would pay all expenses for both him and his spouse, including first-class air fare. I confirmed his attendance by letter, which was sent along with a formal invitation (see Exhibits 11 and 12).

During Expo at Hilton Head, I had several conversations with Milstein. I found him to be bright, friendly, and easy to get along with, although he seemed to have very little information about the business and purchasing aspects of the electronics industry. That made sense when he explained that he was a "techno-geek" with a PhD from MIT, who had worked primarily in research and development at both HP and a now defunct software company, i-Gloo, and thus was new to the marketing, sales, purchasing and manufacturing end of the industry.

After playing a round of golf with Milstein, I had a chance to talk to him specifically about purchasing parts for his business. I told him that due to an increase in silicon prices, it was virtually certain that there would be an industry-wide, 10 percent price hike in the cost of ICPs on March 1, YR-1, so if he thought he would need another shipment of ICPs, he should order them before then. He mentioned that he anticipated needing another shipment to fill an order from a major retailer for his HWCs in the early spring of YR-1.

We also talked about Minicom's September YR-2 order and that I had noticed that Minicom had purchased shipment insurance for that individual order. I told him that the custom in the industry was for companies to have a "blanket" risk-of-loss policy rather than buying insurance for each individual shipment. A blanket policy covered all of the incoming shipments for a company for a lot less money than individual shipment insurance. He seemed surprised to hear about such a thing and said that he would look into getting a policy when he returned home. Because it's true that the blanket policy is cheaper than what they were doing, I was confident that he would purchase such a policy, although I was never told that the blanket policy was in place.

Those are the only two specific conversations about business I can recall, although I'm sure we talked about the ICPs and other parts we sold that might be of use in his HWCs. By the end of Expo, I felt that I had cemented our relationship with Minicom and that they would likely become a long-term customer. There were several other newer customers at Expo, and they too appeared to be pleased with our products and service, and they too seemed likely to become steady customers in the future. Those new repeat accounts were important to me personally, because I was confident they would help out in my being favorably reviewed for the Eastern Region sales manager, a position that, as I mentioned earlier, was coming open in the first half of YR-1.

The next time we heard from Minicom was in the first week of January YR-1, when Virginia told me she had opened and responded to an e-mail from Lubell inquiring about the availability of 100 gross of ICP-73s at the same price as their previous order. Exhibit 16 is a printout of that e-mail, and Exhibit 17 is Virginia's response. As I said earlier, it was typical for Virginia to provide that kind of information to customers, and there was no need for me to be involved. I wouldn't even have looked at the e-mail when it came in; that was Virginia's job. Yes, I see that the e-mail refers to shipping conditions, but that was of small importance as we will ship in any form that the customer requests so long as they make their request clear in their order.

A couple of days later, after a day spent with the higher-ups from New York about the possible promotion, I read an e-mail from Virginia telling me that Lubell had called and that he wanted me to return the call (Exhibit 19). When I asked Virginia to get him on the phone, she told me I didn't need to call him. She said that Lubell had wanted to talk about another order, but that she had told him to send the order in via fax or mail and the fax had come in. Since Lubell had faxed in an order for 100 gross ICP-73s, and it was past normal business hours and I was scheduled for dinner with the interviewing panel, I didn't see a need for me to return the call. I asked Virginia if there was anything unusual about the order, and she said it was standard, so I asked her to process the order. No, I do not believe I read the fax at that time, but I may have. No, it did not call for anything special in terms of handling that I can see.

In processing the order, Virginia followed our normal procedure and sent a work order to the warehouse (Exhibit 21) and followed up with a form thank-you note she signed on my behalf (Exhibit 22) and a statement of account (Exhibit 23). The statement of account clearly shows that there was no insurance on the January YR-1 order.

Yes, I recognize what you have marked as Exhibits 22 A, B, and C from my review of the file. Exhibit 20A is the fax cover sheet of Lubell's order, Exhibit 20B is the fax, and Exhibit 20C is another copy of the order we received by mail. Given my conversation with Virginia, and the hectic atmosphere in the office surrounding my being interviewed for the promotion, I did not actually read the faxed order until sometime in late February or early March, when this dispute arose. Virginia processed the order just as requested by Lubell. I know that Lubell now claims that he asked for insurance on the shipment, but in our industry the custom is, as I had told Milstein, for companies to have blanket risk-of-loss policies, and without a specific request for insurance like what Lubell asked for in September of YR-2, a single shipment insurance policy is not purchased. To do so would mean that the typical customer would end up with double coverage and have to pay for insurance twice.

If I had read the order on January 6 when it came in, my interpretation would have been the same as Virginia's, and no insurance would have been purchased for the shipment. To anyone at BMI or any other company in the industry, the language "per the usual agreement" would have been understood to mean the usual agreement in the industry.

In the middle of January YR-1, we received a return of a shipment of ICP-22s that had been mistakenly sent to Minicom, together with a letter from Lubell (Exhibit 27) that billed us for shipping and insurance on that return and inquired about the shipment of ICP-73s. We paid for the shipping and insurance right away. I wrote back to Lubell to tell him that in the unlikely event that he would ever have to return a shipment to us in the future, we had a blanket risk of loss policy so that there was no need for him to take out an individual shipment policy. I also assured him that the ICP-73s had been shipped to him (Exhibit 28).

I made inquiry about the Mincom shipment to NPS, and although they put a tracer on the shipment of ICP-73s, they eventually had to admit that the shipment had been lost by them. NPS sent us a check for $400 (Exhibit 30), which was the limit of their liability absent a shipment insurance policy or declaration of excess value, and I forwarded the check to Minicom. As I said earlier, we did not take out insurance on the shipment because there was no specific request to do so by Lubell, and in addition, I believed that given my conversation with Milstein, Minicom would have had a blanket policy in effect by the time of the January order.

When I sent Lubell the NPS check in February of YR-1, I told him that we could fill another order of ICP-73s for Minicom and reminded him of the March 1, YR-1, price hike (see Exhibit 29). As it turned out, Minicom did not have a blanket risk-of-loss policy in effect. When Lubell called in response to my letter, I explained to him that no insurance was taken on the shipment because he had not requested it. I also told him that we would have to bill him for the lost shipment. He seemed very upset, but there was nothing I could do about it. He did say that they needed the parts to fill an order of HWCs, and I told him again that we could expedite another shipment to them.

I next got a call from Milstein about the lost order. He asked for me to see if there was any way that we could replace the shipment. I told him that I would check it out with the legal department. I did not tell him that I didn't think it likely that there was anything we could do because I hoped, despite the NPS screw-up, that we could keep Minicom as a customer. To be fair to Milstein, I did forward his request to legal, and they made it clear that it was BMI's position that Minicom owed us for the lost shipment. They provided a letter for me to send to Milstein, which I did (Exhibit 34). The last I heard from Milstein was a rather angry letter he sent to me in March of YR-1 (Exhibit 35), which I forwarded to legal. Eventually BMI brought this lawsuit against Minicom, and I understand that Minicom has sued us as well.

STATEMENT OF VIRGINIA YOUNG

JULY 22, YR-1

My name is Virginia Young. I am twenty-nine years old and have been married to my husband, Dan Macon, for three years. We live at 25 Scott Place in Brookline, Massachusetts. I work as an administrative assistant to Chris Kay, the sales manager for Eastern Subdivision II of BMI. Dan and I have no children yet. Dan works as one of the assistant sales managers under Mr. Kay at BMI.

I grew up in Nita City, Nita, and attended the public schools there. I am one of six children. My parents, all of my siblings and their families, and many aunts, uncles, and cousins all still live in Nita City. My dad is the head coach of the Nita University baseball team in town and has been doing that for the past twenty years. It is fair to say he is well known in Nita City. After I graduated from Nita City High School, I attended Millbrook Community College in Conwell, Nita, and graduated in YR-8 with a BS in sales and marketing. While at Millbrook I attended a job fair, met with a recruiter for BMI, and was offered a position with BMI in their Brookline, Massachusetts, facility. My first position was in a temporary personnel pool that provided administrative and clerical services for people at the sales and distribution center in Brookline. I first met Chris Kay, who was a management trainee, while I had this job. I did a project and some clerical work for him.

In YR-7, when Chris was promoted to deputy sales assistant and was entitled to have a full-time administrative assistant, he asked me to work with him. We have been together ever since. My career has tracked his in that every time he was promoted (from trainee to deputy sales assistant to sales assistant to assistant sales manager to sales manager) he asked me to continue to work with him. As his responsibilities increased, so did mine. And each promotion for him meant a promotion and a raise for me as well. I also received merit raises, when recommended by Mr. Kay, which in my case, has been yearly. My current salary is $48,000 per year.

Chris has risen quickly within the ranks at BMI. He is considered to be on a fast track to senior management. He has been moving up much more quickly than the other people in his management trainee class (the people hired at the same time as him as entry level people). In fact, two assistant sales managers who work under him have been with BMI longer than him, and several people from his management trainee year work under him as sales assistants.

Chris has been in his current job since YR-3, and in early YR-1 he was being considered for a promotion to the position of sales manager for the entire Eastern Region. He told me that if he was offered the position he would like me to come along. That would have meant a raise for me to $60,000 per year. Because that would have meant a move to the regional office in Stamford, Connecticut, he told me that he would try to find a good position for Dan in that office as well. As it turned out, we never had to cross that bridge because Chris did not get that promotion. I am sure he will be promoted in the future, though—he is very good at his job, and a nice man to boot.

Chris is my only supervisor and is responsible for doing my performance evaluations. My evaluations have always been excellent. For the past few years, he has had me fill in "excellent" (the highest rating) in all categories on the evaluation form and give it to him to sign and submit. Chris and I have a great working relationship. Chris has frequently referred to me as his "right arm," and I work very hard to do a good job for him and BMI.

Chris and his wife, Andrea, have always taken good care of me. I have been a guest at his house for holiday parties and other company-related events. In fact, it was Andrea who introduced me to Dan at a holiday party at the Kays' house. Naturally, I am very thankful for that introduction since we married a year later.

As Chris's administrative assistant, I handle his incoming and outgoing correspondence, screen his calls, open and respond to his e-mails, and process orders from our customers. I am also authorized to prepare and sign form letters that go out over Chris's signature when Chris is unavailable. I frequently speak with customers over the phone or via e-mail to provide information regarding the availability of product, price, and shipping and payment conditions. I also handle more personal matters, like keeping his social calendar, making haircut appointments, and getting tee times for him. I also remind him of birthdays and anniversaries. These kinds of tasks are not in my job description, but when Chris asked if I minded helping him out on those kinds of things, I gladly did them because they make him more efficient in his job.

I am not authorized to make contracts for BMI. Chris does that. BMI also has a policy that is made very clear to all of us that it does not take telephone or e-mail orders. We are instructed that when speaking with customers or potential customers to make sure to tell them that when they order to be sure to do so by fax or some other hard copy like USPS. I know that Chris can waive the policy, but he's the only one in the office who can, and I don't remember him ever having done so. BMI's policy about the written form of orders has been in effect since I started with the company. I know that we print it on all of our price lists and brochures and it's on our Web site, and whenever I speak with a customer about a potential order, I always remind them that orders have to be made in hard copy by either fax or USPS.

Although there is no written policy on how I do my job (it is left to the employees with administrative assistants to work out how they will function together), Chris and I have developed a usual way of doing things for routine activities. For outgoing correspondence:

1. Chris will typically dictate a letter using voice recognition software on his computer and e-mail it to me;

2. I then will clean it up and hand it to him in hard copy, and if he isn't in, I place it on his desk chair;

3. Chris then makes any changes that he wants and gives the hard copy back to me;

4. I then prepare the final version for his signature, together with an addressed envelope;

5. Sometimes he will make additional changes, but eventually I will get a signed letter from him. Once that happens, I scan it to our digital files which are in folders on my server drive by the customer's name. That information can be accessed only by Chris or me. I will also distribute any other copies shown on the letter or blind copies. As for the original, I will fold it, place it in the envelope whose address matches the address on the letter, run it through the postage meter, and leave it for pick up by the mail-room people, who take mail to the post office twice a day. Alternatively, if speed is more important than the look of the correspondence, I'll attach a scanned letter to an e-mail. No, we would not accept an order letter scanned into an e-mail. As I was instructed, there is too much of a risk that either the wrong document will be scanned and attached or that no document will be attached at all, either of which would leave uncertainty about the order avoided by requiring a hard copy.

We also have procedures that have been developed for incoming correspondence, whether by fax or mail, as follows:

1. The mail is delivered twice a day at 9:00 a.m. and at 2:00 p.m. Fax correspondence is received throughout the day through the computer on my desk;

2. I open all mail and discard what is obviously junk mail. When in doubt, I keep the piece of mail and follow the next step, which is to stamp the correspondence as received, with the date of receipt;

3. All orders or other important correspondence are scanned to the customer's file after they are stamped as received, and then with other mail is placed on Chris's desk; and

4. After he reviews the orders and mail he will tell me either orally or by placing a "post-it" on the correspondence what to do with each piece of correspondence. Usually he has me do one or more of these things:

   a. digitally file it under the sender's name;

   b. throw it away;

   c. he may prepare a voice-recognition dictated response in the manner I described earlier;

   d. tell me to send a form response; and

   e. in the case of orders, tell me to process the order, which includes preparing a work order based on the written order for the appropriate warehouse (different warehouses handle different products). The work order shows the name of the product and the amount of the product, the address of the customer, and any special shipping conditions such as ship by such-and-such a date. I then prepare a thank-you note and statement of account to be sent to the customer.

The purposes of the thank-you note and statement are to acknowledge the order and notify the client as to when the shipment was sent and how. The statement serves as an invoice to be paid by the client. To be sure that we have actually shipped the product in the amount and manner that the customer desired, the letter asks the customer to inform us if there are any errors in the letter or the statement of account. Our normal shipper is National Parcel Service (NPS).

With regard to e-mail to Chris's BMI business e-mail account, I read the e-mail as it comes in. If the e-mail requires Chris to respond personally, I will forward the e-mail to him. If the e-mail asks for information that is available to me, such as availability of product, pricing, how quickly product can be shipped, or payment terms, I will respond to the e-mail on behalf of Chris. No, I do not copy my responses to Chris; he trusts me to provide accurate information. If the e-mail seeks to place an order or inquires about the availability of product for a potential order, I always remind the customer in my reply of BMI's policy that all orders have to be made by either fax or mail.

The procedure for Chris's outgoing calls is as follows:

1. He will ask me to place a call to a particular person.

2. I will get the number either from our contacts list or an online phone directory and place the call, then:

   a. ask for the party;

   b. get the party on the phone;

c.   ask the party to hold for Mr. Kay;

d.   notify Chris that his party is on the line, and then he takes the call.

3. As a result of the call Chris may have me do a number of things including:

a.   send a letter;

b.   retrieve some information and provide it to the customer, usually by e-mail; or

c.   make a follow-up call.

For incoming calls:

1. I answer the phone saying, "BMI, Mr. Kay's office, Virginia Young speaking. May I help you?"

2. If the party asks for Mr. Kay, I'll get the caller's name and purpose for calling.

3. If the customer wants information that I have, I will provide it; but if the customer still wants to speak with Chris, I'll ask the party to hold to see if Mr. Kay is in.

a.   I notify Chris of the call and ask if he wants to take it; and either

b.   Chris will pick up the call; if he is out or busy, I will take a message, which is sent to Chris via an e-mail. Chris does not like people to have to leave messages on his voice mail, so I always take his messages.

If a customer tries to order one of our products over the phone, which is unusual, I always remind the customer that all orders must be made by fax (and provide the number) or by mail (and provide the address).

I know that we had dealings with Minicom before the one that this lawsuit is about, but I needed to review all the materials that we found when I searched our server for the lawyers to refresh my memory about them. I am told BMI's lawyers gave you everything I found. From the file, I know that we sent a brochure and a price list for integrated chip platforms (ICPs) to Minicom in July of YR-2 (Exhibit 1). Minicom's first order was in September of YR-2. I'm sure I answered the phone and connected the caller with Mr. Kay,   because I always do. I do not remember speaking with anyone from Minicom in September other than to answer the phone. I recognize Exhibits 3A and B as a fax cover sheet and fax order from Minicom; Exhibit 3C as a USPS letter order from Minicom and a copy of the fax; Exhibit 4 is the work order I prepared for that order. Yes, I did have that order insured as the order letter specifically requested us to do so. How Minicom ordered parts in September of YR-2 was certainly not on my mind in January of YR-1. We had processed over a hundred orders between the two from Minicom, and there was no real reason for me to remember the September order in January of the next year. Exhibits 6 and 7 are the thank-you note and statement of account for the September order that I also prepared; and Exhibit 8 is a letter I opened from Minicom containing their payment of our invoice. It was a routine order. The only reason I have any recollection of the details of that first order is from reviewing the materials I collected from our server.

I do remember that Chris was happy about Minicom's new business with us because he decided to invite a Minicom representative to our Expo held in Hilton Head, South Carolina, in December of YR-2. Chris viewed Minicom as a potential long-term account. I handled all of the correspondence for the Expo, which includes Exhibits 11 and 12, but I did not attend.

In January of YR-1, I did open an e-mail sent to Chris from a Mr. Lubell at Minicom making an inquiry about the availability of 100 gross of our ICP 73s. Exhibit 16 is a printout of that e-mail. I responded to that e-mail, saying the parts were available and confirmed the price and payment terms and asked that he place any order by fax or mail. Exhibit 17 is a printout of my response. I have no reason to believe that the e-mail exchange did not occur on January 3, YR-1, as shown on the e-mail.

I don't know whether I said anything to Chris about the e-mail. During the beginning of January, Chris was extremely busy preparing for a visit from head-office management, who were coming to Brookline to evaluate our facility and to interview Chris for the promotion to sales manager for the Eastern Region that I mentioned earlier. As a result, things were very hectic, and I doubt that I would have thought it important enough to show Chris the routine e-mail exchange.

A couple of days later, on January 6, YR-1, I answered a phone call from Mr. Lubell at Minicom. I remember the call because after I informed him that Chris was unavailable and asked if I could help him, he tried to place an order for parts over the phone. Although I do not recall what I said specifically, I am sure that I told him that his order had to be placed by fax or mail because that is what I always do. There is no chance that I took his order over the phone. That is something I would never do.

I do not remember whether Mr. Lubell mentioned that he wanted to have his order insured, but I think if he had made such a request I would have remembered it because it would have been an extremely rare request. As I understand it, most companies we deal with have a blanket insurance policy that covers all shipments we make to them, and my clear instruction from Chris, for as long as I have been processing orders for him at BMI, is not to insure a shipment and bill the customer for the insurance unless there is a specific written request from the customer for insurance. But no, I cannot swear that he did not mention insurance. That's because what we go by is the written order, so any terms he mentioned over the phone wouldn't have been important to me. As Chris explained many years ago, the customer can always change his mind after the fact about orders, so we always go by the writing.

The day that Mr. Lubell called we got a fax order from Minicom. Exhibit 20A is the fax cover sheet, and 20B is the fax order. We also got a letter order by USPS several days later, which is Exhibit 20C. I don't know why he sent both a fax and a letter—either one would have been sufficient. You are right that the cover sheet says that the letter is "confirming Minicom's phone order," but I do not attach any meaning to that language. The fax was the order, and since we had it, there was no reason to quarrel with Mr. Lubell's characterization as it confirming anything. It certainly would not change the way the order was processed. Frankly, I don't know that I noticed the "confirming" language when the fax came in. It was the order that was important. I do not remember whether Chris read the fax or letter order; probably not. I believe that because he was so busy I just told him that an order came in and that he told me to process the order, which I did.

Looking at the fax order and the letter order, which are identical, I would never take the order to be one requesting insurance. I know that is what Minicom claims it does, but "the usual agreement" is, as I explained earlier, not to take out insurance unless there is a specific request to do so, and the request just isn't there. I handled this order just like I handle any other order to BMI. Anyhow, if what Mr. Lubell wanted was insurance, he should have called to tell us that there was an error in his statement of account like the thank-you note asks the customer to do if there is an error in the statement. Exhibits 22 and 23 are the thank-you note and the statement. If he had called and made it clear that he wanted insurance, I would have made sure he got it because their order hadn't been shipped until after he got our letter; and it does not bill for insurance, because he didn't ask for it.

That was really the last I had to do with Minicom, other than referring calls to Mr. Kay, opening correspondence from them, and preparing correspondence to them. I do remember that Minicom sent us back a shipment of ICPs that was mistakenly sent to them by the warehouse. It is unusual for the warehouse to make such a mistake, but mistakes do happen from time to time.

Naturally, I had some conversations with Chris about the lost shipment back when it happened, but I did not say anything to him that I haven't told you. Those conversations were before this lawsuit started. Since then, we have not spoken about the case on the advice of our lawyer.

MATERIALS AVAILABLE
ONLY TO THE DEFENDANT'S LAW FIRM
(MINICOM'S COUNSEL)

STATEMENT OF MICHAEL LUBELL

AUGUST 17, YR-1

My name is Michael Lubell, and I live at 214 Burning Tree Drive in Nita City, Nita. I am thirty-one years old, and I am married to the former Ellen Scheps. We have no children, but hope to start a family in the not too distant future. We met when I was a student at MIT and she was attending Harvard. I was introduced to Ellen by my roommate at the time, Elliot Milstein, and his then girlfriend, now wife, Zoe. Zoe and Ellen were best friends. Ellen and I actually grew up in the same part of Connecticut, although we had never met before college. I had graduated from Lyman Hall High School in Wallingford, and Ellen, whose family lived in neighboring Cheshire, actually went to prep school at Choate Rosemary Hall, which is located in Wallingford. We were married the summer after graduation from college in YR-10, the same summer that Elliot and Zoe got married. We have been good friends with the Milsteins since our days in college.

Ellen is a medical doctor with a specialty in internal medicine. She received her MD in YR-7 from Tufts University, and finished her residency and fellowship at Massachusetts General Hospital in YR-3. She is on staff at Nita University Medical Center and serves on the Medical School faculty as an Assistant Professor of Medicine.

After graduating from MIT with a degree in computer science, I enrolled in the MBA program at Boston University. I was accepted into the program without any previous business experience (which I was told by the school was unusual) only because of my expertise in the computer field, which the school viewed as a substitute for experience in the business community, at least with regard to information technology. The program was a two-year program, but even though I was in the top quarter of my class and in good academic standing, I left after one year in YR-9 because it was really geared for someone who wanted a career on Wall Street, and that wasn't me. I decided that I would apply to law school, so while I completed applications, I worked for Apple at the Genius Bar in one of their retail outlets in Boston troubleshooting their products, apps, and software.

In YR-8, I was accepted into the JD program at Northeastern University School of Law and started that fall. I hated law school almost immediately, but stuck it out through the first year. I was doing fine academically. Northeastern does not have a traditional grading system, but I was in good standing. I left after exams in May YR-7 and decided to look for something else to do, but I could have gone back to Northeastern if I wanted to. For the next year, I worked as a paralegal in the patents department of the Smith, Liu & Roberts law firm in Boston. The pay was good, and we needed the income to help pay for Ellen's medical school education, but I found the work tedious.

In the late spring of YR-6, a friend of mine from BU, John Staffier, approached me with a proposal to open up an electronics retail business specializing in high-end computer games, hardware and games for Wii, Xbox, and PlayStation systems, and software geared toward the sophisticated student market. He had what he called a prime location in Cambridge, and by September of YR-5, with loans from my parents and John's parents, we opened our store, called Techno-Toys. The shop was an instant success, and we were able to pay off the parental loans with a line of credit provided by the bank. We did very well until a big box store opened up around the corner from us and essentially covered our market. With their volume sales pricing, they eventually drove us out of business.

By January of YR-4, we were out of business and into bankruptcy. While we were in the process of losing our business, I did something stupid. When our credit line ran out, I wrote some personal checks to try to restock our shop, and the checks bounced. I had hoped that sales would cover the checks, but that didn't work out. When I couldn't pay the checks (I was too proud to ask my parents for help), I was arrested and charged with larceny. Because the amount involved was over $4,000, it was a felony with up to two years in jail possible. My parents paid for a lawyer, who got me a deal. I pled guilty because I was guilty and got a one-year suspended sentence with two years probation. As a condition of my probation, I had to pay a fine, court costs, and restitution. The restitution was to pay back all the checks with interest. I successfully completed my probation without any problems, having paid back everything with interest.

From February of YR-4 until May of YR-3, I worked as a sales clerk at a Verizon kiosk at CambridgeSide Galleria in Cambridge while Ellen was finishing her fellowship at Mass. General. We had agreed that when she completed her fellowship, we would move to wherever she received her best offer, so it didn't make much sense for me to try to find a career-type position. I tried to get my old job back at the law firm, but the conviction was a problem for them, so I just worked in retail sales for Verizon while I made enough to pay off the bad checks.

As it turned out, we ended up in Nita City for two reasons. First, Ellen got a great offer to go on staff and on faculty at Nita University's med school and Memorial Hospital. Second, I got offered a position at Minicom by Elliot Milstein.

We had remained very friendly with the Milsteins after graduating from college. For the first three years, Elliot was in a PhD program in electrical engineering at MIT. Zoe, who was an economics major, got her MBA from Harvard and worked for a year in an investment house in Boston. In YR-7, they moved to northern New Jersey, where Elliot worked for HP in research and design for two years while Zoe worked on Wall Street. In YR-5, Elliot went with a start-up software company named i-Gloo (also located in northern New Jersey), which eventually went public. He cashed in his stock options in late YR-4, and he and Zoe moved back to their hometown, Nita City. They wanted to start a family, and they wanted to be near their families in Nita City.

During the time we were all in Boston after graduation, we saw the Milsteins probably twice a month for dinner or a movie or something. After they moved to New Jersey, we would talk on the phone or e-mail on a regular basis, and each summer we would get a place on the New Jersey shore for a week. I would say that Elliot is probably my best friend, and I think Ellen would say the same about Zoe.

In the early winter of YR-3, just as Ellen was trying to figure out which position she would take after her fellowship, I got a call from Elliot, and he told me that he was going to start his own company, called Minicom. It was his idea to design and manufacture a very sophisticated handheld wearable computer known as an HWC. He already had the design completed and was working on demonstration models. Similar to a high-end phone, but higher tech and much sturdier, Elliot's HWC operated as a computer with Internet capability, an MP3 player, video player, a phone, a GPS, got TV reception, took still photos and video, played computer games, acted as a PDA, and then some. Its flexibility (it could be bent or dropped without being hurt) made it extremely sturdy for use by people both in their day-to-day living and while engaging in such outdoor activities as skiing, hiking, boating, etc. Elliot was very excited about the design's prospects and had already obtained a lease on a warehouse on Science Drive in the Research Park in Nita City. The facility was being renovated, and he hoped to be up and running by the late fall of YR-3.

Elliot said that he needed someone who could act as his Vice President for Purchasing. He said the job involved buying all the products and services that Minicom needed. He said that he thought of me because of my knowledge of computers and said that because of my business school and law school experience he thought I would be a great contracting agent for his company. I reminded Elliot about my bad checks problem, which he knew all about from one night in the summer of YR-4 while we were on vacation when I had a bunch to drink and confided in him. Elliot said that he knew who I was at heart, that he trusted me, and that if he had any problems with the conviction he would not have made the offer.

Elliot also told me that he had persuaded a number of other people he knew from previous experiences to join the management team. Charles Bentley from MIT was the VP for Manufacturing, Debbie Silver, whom Zoe knew from her Wall Street days, was the CFO and VP for Finance, and Larry Schwartz, whom Elliot knew from i-Gloo, was the VP for Marketing.

Elliot said that he had decided to use his cash-out from i-Gloo and some of Zoe's bonus money from Wall Street to build a future for his family. I later learned that he also got a line of credit for financing based on guarantees from his parents and Zoe's folks. Ellen joined us when Zoe got on the phone, and we found out Zoe was pregnant with their first child, who was due in late July of YR-3. We couldn't have been happier for them, and about a month later, when Ellen got her offer from Nita University Memorial, we decided to make the move to Nita City.

I was very much looking forward to the Minicom job. The way Elliot had set up the company, all the VPs came on for a base salary of $45,000 per year. The other VPs took a pay cut, but because I was biding time waiting for Ellen's career move when the offer came in, it was actually a $10,000 raise for me over my Verizon job, but not what I could have earned on the open market. In addition to the base salary, Elliot created a profit-sharing plan whereby he would receive 60 percent of the profits of the business, each VP would receive a guarantee of 5 percent of the profits, and the remainder of the profits would be divided by all the employees of the company (VPs included) based on their years of service at Minicom. It was also anticipated that at some point Minicom would go public, and there would be stock options for the four VPs.

Ellen's job started in June of YR-3, so we moved to our current condo then. The renovations on the Science Drive facility took longer than expected, so that delayed the official opening of the business. Elliot continued work on his designs and demo models for the HWC out of his home. Debbie, Larry, and Charles delayed their move to Nita City until we opened up in January of YR-2. I spent that summer and fall setting up the condo and doing some minor renovations. I would also spend time with Elliot at his house talking about Minicom and admiring his and Zoe's new son, Jake, who was born in late July.

When we opened in January, Charles and Elliot spent time working on design and demo models, while Debbie set up the financial side of the business and Larry started working on marketing plans. As work progressed, Elliot hired people as needed in the manufacturing/assembly plant that was also located at the Science Drive location. We now have a total work staff, including the VPs and Elliot, of twenty-two people. My job was to buy everything we needed. I worked with vendors buying things from office supplies and desks to computer parts and other items necessary for assembling our HWCs. I also spent some time getting to know the industry. While our HWCs were a unique product, they were assembled with the use of a number of parts that were manufactured by much larger companies; BMI was one.

Because of our size, we had no written procedures for how orders of products were made at Minicom, so I sort of figured it out as I went along. The formality of the ordering process I used depended in large part on the expense involved. Relatively inexpensive items like office supplies and the like were typically ordered by phone or e-mail, or sometimes in person. For more expensive items, like component parts for our demo HWCs that cost thousands of dollars, many companies required that we fill out written order forms prepared by them, but that was not universal. Other suppliers of expensive items would take an order over the phone or via e-mail as long as there was a written confirmation of the order. The bottom line was that we would conform to the processes expected by the supplier of the products we ordered. Generally, it is fair to say that for most suppliers, the formality of the process lessened with the frequency of purchases by us.

The only firm policy Minicom had was that on any purchase over $2,500 shipped to us we required insurance to protect us against the shipment being lost or damaged. I would request the supplier to procure the insurance either as a "shipment policy" or, in the case of shippers such as UPS, by declaring what is called "excess valuation" for the shipment, which meant that they automatically charged for insurance, which they provided. Shipment policies or declaring excess valuation was necessary because shippers all limit their liability by the terms of their shipping contract. Given the size and number of shipments we were receiving, we had insufficient volume as of the summer and even into the fall of YR-2 to procure an insurance policy that would automatically insure all of our orders. I know I mentioned to Elliot that once we got into a major production run, we should look into what is commonly known as a "blanket" risk-of-loss shipping insurance policy.

By the late summer of YR-2, Larry Schwartz had procured a number of orders for stripped-down versions of our HWCs and was working on finding a major retailer for our product so that tie-ins with service providers like Verizon or ATT could be made. Up until then, we had been purchasing the component parts for our demo HWCs from independent jobbers or middlemen because we had no need for the sort of volume orders required for purchases directly from manufacturers of those parts. In August of YR-2, in anticipation of our first major production run, Elliot asked me to order a number of the component parts used in our HWCs in amounts sufficient to fill our order. That kind of bulk purchasing allowed me to go directly to the manufacturers and get much better pricing on the parts than we were receiving from the middlemen.

One component we needed in high volume was an integrated chip platform, usually referred to as an ICP. Manufacturers of ICPs typically sell them in minimum lots of one gross. There are 144 parts in a gross. In our base model HWC, two ICPs are used in each unit. For that first production run, which was for a little over 6,000 units, we decided to order 100 gross of the ICPs to account for faulty platforms or damage in storage or assembly. Because I had been surveying the potential suppliers for known component parts, I knew that there were not many companies that manufactured ICPs. BMI was one of those suppliers, and in fact they had sent us a brochure and a price list for ICPs earlier in the summer of YR-2. Exhibit 1 looks like the price list I received from BMI. As I told my lawyer, I couldn't find the actual one sent to us in our files, but I do remember receiving a price list from them in the summer of YR-2.

When I started calling about the pricing and availability of product, I found that the pricing for the part we needed (ICPs come with differing technical characteristics) was remarkably similar across suppliers. The last supplier I contacted was BMI, and I was directed by their information line to their closest distribution facility, which was in Brookline, Massachusetts. The person I spoke with at BMI was Chris Kay. That was on September 3, YR-2. Exhibit 2 is a printout of my computerized phone log that shows that call. We had a policy at Minicom to fill out phone logs for all outgoing and incoming calls on a form on our computers. The data was filled in and stored electronically. The way I filled out the outgoing log was to input the date, the person or company called, and the phone number as I was making the call, and then fill in the business purpose column either while on the phone (I use a headset at work to keep my hands free) or right after the call. This log gives us a pretty reliable record of our calls and their content.

Kay and I spoke about the technical requirements that we had for ICPs, and we determined that the platform we needed to order was BMI's part number ICP-73. Kay quoted a price of $5,000 per gross, which was acceptable to us, and confirmed that he had 100 gross available for immediate shipment. Because BMI had the earliest availability and everyone's prices seem to be pretty much the same, I decided to go with BMI. Kay and I talked about the terms of the order and agreed to the price for 100 gross that he quoted, that the parts would be shipped within ten days via NPS, that BMI would procure shipment insurance or declare excess valuation, and that the payment terms would include a discount of two percent for payment within thirty days. Once we had reached an agreement, Kay thanked me for my order, but said that he needed a confirming letter by fax and mail. I was more than willing to provide him with the writing, especially because when first dealing with a company it was good to set out in detail the terms of how you would be doing business with them, especially when, as with BMI, we anticipated future dealings.

Exhibits 3A and B are the fax cover sheet and fax letter. Exhibit 3C appears to be the letter I mailed. The parts were received, and according to Elliot and Charles Bentley, they were technically acceptable with a very low defect rate. Kay had sent me a letter and a bill for the September order (Exhibits 6 and 7), and we paid it by check in time to receive the discount. Exhibit 8 is my cover letter that I sent with the check, which is Exhibit 9.

That was the last I had to do with BMI until January of YR-1. BMI did, however, invite Elliot and Zoe to an all-expense paid exposition in Hilton Head, South Carolina, in December of YR-2. Elliot got back from the Expo about the time I was leaving for a holiday break, so I didn't really get a chance to talk to him, but I did get an e-mail from him telling me to make another order of ICPs from BMI after the first of the year. Exhibit 14 is a printout of that e-mail. I knew that Larry Schwartz had persuaded Neiman Marcus to order 5,000 units of a more sophisticated HWC that used three ICPs per unit. Together with what was left over from the first ICP order, I determined we needed another 100 gross of platforms. Elliot also said in the e-mail that Kay had told him that there was an industry-wide price hike of 10 percent coming in March of YR-1 and asked that I check out a rumor he had heard about some sort of price-fixing investigation that he thought might be involved in the price hike.

I had read about the price hike which was due to some materials costs increases, but when I called the Department of Justice in early January to check out the rumor, their information officer would neither confirm nor deny that there was an ongoing investigation. I will say that he didn't seem surprised by the question, so I assumed there was one going on, but as far as I know nothing came of the investigation.

I returned from my holiday break (which we spent first in Connecticut with Ellen's parents and then in Florida with my parents) right before New Year's Day of YR-1. Right after the first of January, I got an e-mail from Elliot informing me that he had purchased a blanket risk-of-loss policy to cover all of our incoming shipments based on a tip he got in Hilton Head. Exhibit 15 is a printout of that e-mail. I guess he forgot that I had suggested to him that we investigate blanket policies as early as the fall of YR-2 when we started making bulk orders of component parts for our HWCs. I was a little surprised that he purchased the policy himself as he usually relies on me to purchase services as well as products, but it's his company, and he can do what he wants. The policy was not going into effect until February 1, so I continued our policy of insuring purchases individually until then.

On January 3, YR-1, I sent an e-mail to Kay at BMI to inquire about another shipment of ICP-73s. Exhibit 16 is a printed version of that e-mail. I wanted to find out about availability of the platforms and to confirm the price and shipping conditions that were available in September of YR-2. By shipping conditions, I meant shipment within ten days, using NPS, and with insurance. Kay didn't respond, but a Virginia Young did on his behalf. Exhibit 17 is a printed version of that response. She apparently hadn't read my e-mail carefully because she didn't address the shipping conditions at all.

On January 6, YR-1, I placed a call to Kay. A person identifying herself as Virginia Young and as being Kay's assistant answered the phone. I assumed it was the same Virginia Young who had responded to my e-mail. It turned out that Kay wasn't available to take my call, so I gave our order to Young, telling her I wanted 100 gross of ICP-73s for $500,000, that I wanted them shipped within ten days by NPS, and that I wanted them insured. She said that was fine and asked for a confirming letter. Exhibit 18 is a printout of my computerized phone log for January 6, YR-1, that has the entry for that call. I also asked Young to have Kay give me a call, and she took my phone number. Kay never called.

Within an hour or so of that call I faxed the letter confirming the agreement I had made with BMI and referred specifically to the phone call agreement in both the fax cover sheet (Exhibit 20A) and the fax letter (Exhibit 20B). Exhibit 20C is the USPS letter that they also asked for, but it is identical to the fax. To be clear about what I wanted, I specifically referred to my call with Young and our agreement on the phone, and I also stated in the confirmation that I wanted the order to be handled as per the usual agreement that we had with BMI. We had only one other agreement, so I don't know how they screwed up and didn't take out insurance.

I did get a letter signed by Young for Kay and a bill a little over a week later on January 14, YR-1 (Exhibits 22 and 23). Whether I read the bill carefully or not the day it came in, I can't say. The letter asked to be sure the parts were satisfactory. Since we hadn't gotten them by the time of the letter, I could not respond at that time. I do know that several days later we got a package from BMI. The shipping record (Exhibit 25) showed that it contained ten gross of ICP-73s, but when it was opened we found ten gross of their part number ICP-22. When I sent that mistaken order back to BMI, I insured the parts and sent a letter explaining the reason for return and correcting the bill that they had sent us that failed to charge us for insurance (Exhibit 27). I also told Kay in the letter that we really needed the shipment by January 31, YR-1, to fill our Neiman Marcus order.

A week later, I got a letter from Kay saying that the ICP-73s we had ordered were sent out on January 16 and that he was tracing the order with NPS. He did not mention anything about the fact they had not billed us for insurance or anything about getting the parts to us by January 31, when they were needed. Exhibit 28 is Kay's letter.

The second week in February, Elliot told me that we were running low on ICPs, and I told him that the shipment had been delayed but Kay was looking into it. I remember calling Kay's office from home several times because I was out with the flu, but he did not respond to me. On February 18, YR-1, I got a letter from Kay (Exhibit 29) saying that NPS had lost the parts. The letter contained a $400 NPS check, which he said was NPS's limit of liability. He also said that he could fill another order of ICPs. I immediately called Kay and asked him whether the shipment insurance on the shipment had paid BMI for the lost parts or whether the insurance check would come to us. Kay said there was no insurance and that we hadn't asked for insurance. I was adamant that we had and went over the phone call with his assistant and the confirming letter. He said there was nothing he could do. Exhibit 31 is a printout of my phone log that records that call.

Yes, I am on medication today. I have a prescription for Paxil from my doctor that I take for anxiety during periods when I am under a lot of stress. The last time that I used the Paxil before BMI lost the shipment was around the time that my store was going out of business and I had that trouble with the law. I did start taking it again since Kay's call. This whole BMI mess has had me very worried. No, I was not taking Paxil when I made the order of ICPs from BMI in January. I had just gotten back from a very relaxing vacation, and there was nothing particularly stressful happening in my life in that time period. Even if I had been, Paxil does not affect my ability to function at a high level at my job; in fact, when I am anxious it helps me concentrate.

After Kay's call, I reviewed my phone log, e-mails, faxes, and correspondence regarding the order and was convinced that BMI had screwed up our order. Elliot was out of the office, so I sent him an e-mail suggesting that since he had dealt with Kay personally in Hilton Head that perhaps he could get Kay to replace the shipment that they had failed to insure. Exhibit 32 is a printed version of that e-mail. Elliot reviewed my records and agreed that it was a BMI screw-up. I know that he called Kay and was hopeful that the parts would be replaced, but as it turned out, Kay eventually refused to do so. That was sometime after the first week of March.

Once Elliot heard that BMI was not going to make good on their mistake, Elliot told me to order the replacement ICPs from another supplier. I did so from Exrox. Exhibit 37 is a copy of my e-mail order for those parts. Exhibits 38 and 39 are Exrox's acknowledgement of the order and their bill. Exhibit 42 is a second bill we got from them when we were unable to make timely payment to them.

As it turned out, there were some problems with the Exrox platform in that they were configured in a slightly different way than BMI's parts and that required some minor, but necessary, design modifications. That, in addition to BMI's screw up, further delayed the production of our order for Neiman Marcus, so they pulled the plug on the deal when we couldn't promise delivery of their entire order by their deadline.

I'll admit that I felt very bad that all of this happened and that for a while in March of YR-1 I was having some problems at work. I even considered leaving Minicom and made a few inquiries. At some point in early April, Elliot came down to see me and told me to get over it, that we would make do, but that if my work didn't get back to normal that he would have to replace me. I'm happy to say that I've been able to get back to normal and that business seems to be picking up again. I can't say whether we will turn a profit this year; that would be a question for Elliot or Debbie Silver. I do know that we are not so flush that the $500,000 BMI is suing us for wouldn't really hurt.

STATEMENT OF ELLIOT MILSTEIN

AUGUST 17, YR-1

My name is Elliot Milstein. I am thirty-two years old, married to my wife of ten years, Zoe, and we have a two-year-old son named Jake. Zoe and I met while we were in high school in Nita City and became a couple when we were in college. In YR-10, she graduated from Harvard, and I graduated from MIT. We were married that summer. We live at 32 Whitehead Circle in Nita City, Nita.

My undergraduate degree at MIT was in electrical engineering. After graduation, I enrolled in a PhD program in electrical engineering with an emphasis in computer science, from which I graduated in YR-7. While I was in that graduate program, Zoe received her MBA from Harvard in YR-8 and then worked in a financial services firm in Boston.

In YR-7, I took a job in research and development with HP in their Ridgefield, New Jersey, facility. Zoe went to work on Wall Street as a financial analyst, where she was employed until YR-4. I left HP for a software company called i-Gloo in YR-5. I was very fortunate that the company took off and went public, and I received a significant number of stock options. By late YR-4, I became worried about the viability of i-Gloo. It seemed that the quality of our marketing was far exceeding the quality of our products. That, together with the fact that we wanted to start a family and that I had always wanted to be my own boss, caused me to cash in my stock options in December of YR-4 and move back to Nita City, which was home to both Zoe and myself. Both sets of our parents still live in downtown Nita City. I have no siblings, but Zoe has three older sisters, all of whom are married with kids and live in Nita City's suburbs. Zoe's sisters had all taken some time away from their careers to start their families, but by then Myra, a school principal married to a banker; Leslie, a research chemist for Nita Biotechnics married to a lawyer; and Katie, an art gallery manager married to a graphic artist, were back in the work force. Zoe and I wanted to move home so that our kids would have their aunts, uncles, cousins, and grandparents in their lives.

As it turned out, I was right about i-Gloo, and by the late summer of YR-3, they were out of business, and it was fortunate that we decided to make the move when we did. During January of YR-3, I finished designing a product now known as a handheld wearable computer (HWC) that I had been working on, on my own, for a couple of years. An HWC, like a top end phone or a mini-tablet, combines various technologies and apps in a convenient and manageable size. The HWC product I designed could range from a very basic model having only music and internet capabilities to more sophisticated models with phone, music, photo and HD video recording, GPS, PDA, gaming, video playback, and digital storage. The difference between the product that I designed and others on the market was that mine was sturdier and less bulky than the others as well as completely waterproof and therefore usable by people while they were engaged in outdoor activities like skiing, camping, hiking, boating, and the like. My design made all the conveniences of modern digital life available in virtually any setting.

Zoe, who by that time was pregnant with Jake and was not working, created a business plan for the manufacture, assembly, and marketing of my designs. We decided that rather than taking my designs to a large manufacturer, we should start our own company, which we named Minicom. Our start-up was funded by the proceeds from the i-Gloo stock options plus most of our savings, which had come largely from Zoe's bonuses from her previous positions on Wall Street. We also obtained a substantial line of credit with the Nita National Bank based on guarantees signed by both sets of parents. By the early winter of YR-3, my plans were coming together. I found a warehouse on Science Drive in the Nita Research Park that was the right size for my operation, but was in need of renovation. I obtained a long-term lease, and we began renovations. I also started to assemble my management team.

Zoe and I were interested in bringing people to the company who we liked and could trust and who were willing to invest their time and talent in a new enterprise. We were looking for four management-level people, who we called vice presidents. Debbie Silver was a friend and co-worker of Zoe's from Wall Street. She was also a specialist in taking companies public, which was our long-term goal for Minicom. Because she was looking to make her life less hectic and believed in our business plan, she came aboard as the CFO and VP for Finance. Larry Schwartz had worked as the deputy director of marketing at i-Gloo and was my closest friend from there. We recognized the problems at i-Gloo at about the same time, and he cashed out in January of YR-3. He became our VP for Marketing and Sales. Charles Bentley was a friend of mine from the MIT graduate program. He had become disenchanted with the large companies he had been working with, and he came on as our VP for Manufacturing.

The last position we needed to fill was for a contracting/purchasing agent for the company. We called the position VP for Purchasing. My oldest and best friend from MIT is Mike Lubell. He was my undergraduate roommate. During college, Zoe introduced Mike to his now wife Ellen, who was a college classmate of hers at Harvard, and we have been close to them for almost fifteen years. Mike was a computer science major at MIT. While not the best student, probably because he wasn't as interested in the curriculum as he might have been, Mike certainly was extremely bright, articulate and intellectually facile and curious with varied interests and a lot of info about a lot of things

After graduating from MIT, Mike thought that business school would interest him and he enrolled in Boston University's MBA program. I know he was doing well there academically, but after a year he decided that he wasn't interested in a Wall Street career and left the program. For the next year he worked at the Genius Bar at an Apple store while he applied to law school. He eventually was accepted at Northeastern and started law school in YR-8. Almost from the beginning he disliked law school. Because he was bright, he did well his first year, but that summer he decided that life as a law student was not for him. He must have learned something, however, because he went to work as a paralegal for a large law firm in Boston that did patent work. In that way he used both his MIT and law school learning in his work. Mike made it clear to me that he was only doing the job because the pay was good and he needed to help support Ellen's education (she was in med school at Tufts).

It was at about this time that I finished my degree at MIT, and Zoe and I moved to northern New Jersey where I worked for i-Gloo and Zoe worked on Wall Street. While we were still in the Boston area, we would see Mike and Ellen at least two or three times a month. After we moved away, we mostly communicated by phone and e-mail, but we made it a point to vacation together for a week each summer at the New Jersey shore.

In the late spring of YR-6, Mike was approached by a friend of his from business school, John Staffier, to go in with him on a retail electronic gaming shop in Cambridge, which they called Techno-Toys. Although I felt that Mike could have done better than running a games store, he seemed to enjoy his work and the independence it gave him. The store, which had a great location near thousands of undergraduate students, also did very well until the fall of YR-5, when a big box electronics store opened in the area, selling many of the same products as Techno-Toys with a volume discount and essentially running them out of business. They closed and went into bankruptcy in January of YR-4.

That process was really hard on Mike. He frantically tried to save his business. I later learned that he ended up writing personal checks for the business that bounced, and when he couldn't pay the checks, he pled guilty to something minor relating to the bad checks. I wish Mike had come to me. The amount of the bad checks was just a few thousand dollars, and we would have lent it to him, but he was too proud. I didn't find out about the problems with the law until that summer, when on vacation Mike and I were up late with a little too much to drink and he unburdened himself. I also know that he made good on every one of those checks because it was the right thing to do.

Zoe and I knew that it was the Lubells' intention that when Ellen finished the fellowship she had at Massachusetts General Hospital in YR-3, their next move would be governed by where Ellen wanted to start her practice. For that reason, Mike wasn't able to get a career-oriented job, and he ended up working at the Verizon store in a local mall doing retail sales while waiting for Ellen to finish her program.

Both Zoe and I thought that Mike would be perfect as our VP for Purchasing. He knew the basic technical aspects of digital equipment design necessary to procure parts, and he had graduate work in business and law, which we thought would be of assistance in serving as Minicom's contracting agent. No, I was not concerned about the bad checks problem. That was old news, and in my view an aberration. In February of YR-3, we were ready to tell Mike and Ellen about our pregnancy, and we decided to offer Mike the position at Minicom in the same phone call. The timing was especially right because Ellen was in the process of interviewing for her next career move, and we knew that the University of Nita Medical School and Nita Memorial Hospital were on her list.

I told Mike about our plans, about the VPs we had taken on, and asked him to join us. Mike seemed very interested. When Ellen was offered a position in internal medicine at Nita Memorial and a faculty position at Nita University Med School, Mike agreed to come onboard. Because Ellen's position started in June of YR-3, they moved into a condo at that time. The renovations on the Science Drive facility were going slowly so Minicom did not officially open until January of YR-2. Mike kept himself busy doing some renovations of his own on their condo. He also spent time with me talking about Minicom, going over to the warehouse to check on those renovations, and once Jake was born on July 22, YR-3, being appropriately adoring of him.

When the renovation finally was completed in December of YR-3, we set the formal opening date at January 3, YR-2. Debbie, Larry, and Charles moved to Nita City right around then, and we opened. At first, the only people working were the five of us on the management team and a couple of administrative assistants, who we shared. The management team, recognizing our start-up situation, all agreed to draw a salary of only $45,000 each per year. For everyone except Mike, who because of his family situation was delaying a career move and working for Verizon, the salary was much lower than what they had been making. The way we set up Minicom, however, there was the potential for a large financial reward for all of us in the future if the business took off. As I said, my ultimate goal was to go public, at which point stock options for the management team would have great value. But until that time, our deal was that once there were profits, I would receive 60 percent of the profits, each of the VPs would receive 5 percent of the profits, and the remaining 20 percent to be divided among all of Minicom's employees (including the VPs) according to a formula based on their years of service at Minicom. We have added employees as necessary, and our total work force, including management, is now twenty-two people, most of whom work assembling our products.

During the spring and early summer of YR-2, Charles and I worked on finalizing my designs and building demo models of our line of HWCs. Debbie went about setting up the company's finances. Mike made sure we had all of the materials necessary for our demo line and literally bought every product and service we needed, and Larry started to work on marketing our products.

In late summer of YR-2, Larry had had some success in marketing the lower end HWCs in our product line, and we contracted to provide 6,000 units to various specialty retailers by the end of the year. Although the design of our HWC line was mine with some assistance from Charles, all the component parts that go into our product are designed and manufactured elsewhere. Up until the summer of YR-2, we had been purchasing relatively small quantities of those parts from jobbers as our designs evolved. That summer I learned from a friend who still worked at HP that we could get enormous savings by purchasing many of those parts from manufacturers in bulk. One such part is the integrated chip platform known in the industry as an ICP, which is an electronic component containing chips with electronic operating instructions that allow a number of functionalities to operate at the same time. Once we had our orders in place I asked Mike to investigate making a bulk purchase of ICPs and other component parts for our HWCs.

After some checking around, Mike confirmed that there were lower prices per unit for bulk purchases and learned that the ICPs, for example, were normally sold in lots of one gross. A gross is 144 parts. Because each of the 6,000 base model HWCs involved in that first order utilized two ICPs per unit, we decided to purchase 100 gross to account for part failure, and damage during assembly or storage. We eventually decided to go with BMI as our ICP supplier and ordered a 100 gross of their ICP-73 for $500,000 in early September of YR-2. The parts were received in a timely way and were of exceptional quality.

In November of YR-2, I got a call from a Chris Kay at BMI, who identified himself as the sales manager for them who had dealt with us in our ICP order. Exhibit 10 is my phone log showing that call. At Minicom, all of the managers keep a computer log of both their incoming and outgoing phone calls. It's one of the few set procedures we have and insures we have decent records regarding oral business communications. When he called, Kay invited me to a BMI Expo in Hilton Head, South Carolina, in December. He explained that it was an all-expense paid trip for me and a guest, and that in addition to getting to meet other people in the electronic industry, there would be plenty of time for recreation. I decided to accept the invitation for two reasons. First, Zoe and I had not had a vacation since Jake had been born. Second, at Minicom we were long on enthusiasm, but short on business experience, and I thought that it was important for me to learn what I could from such an opportunity. At first, my only responsibility at Minicom was on the technical end, but as time went on it became clear that I needed to have a better understanding of the industry that we were operating in.

The Hilton Head trip was very pleasant. The weather was a lot better than in Nita City, and we got in some fishing, hiking, and golf, all of which we enjoyed. I also got to meet a number of people in the electronics business. Some of them were relative newcomers like me, working in start-up companies, but others were very experienced and working in well-established companies. And of course, there were the BMI people, who seemed genuinely interested in developing a good relationship with us.

As I said, Kay was the one who invited us. Apparently, Minicom is in his region for BMI. Although he was obviously there to hustle business, he seemed to be a friendly guy. I had a number of conversations with him, but other than talking generally about the business climate and the market for electronics, he really only gave me two specific business tips. The first tip was that there was a materials cost increase that was going to cause an industry-wide price hike of 10 percent for ICPs in March of YR-1, so depending on our needs, we should try to beat the increase. The second tip related to the fact that he had noticed that we had purchased an insurance policy for the shipment of ICPs in September for that one shipment alone. I knew we had done that because we always insured our incoming shipments that cost more than $2,500 against loss or damage, and according to Mike, even though it didn't make a lot of sense to me, losses and damage by the shipper were limited by the shipper and were the responsibility of the buyer as opposed to the seller. Kay's tip about this was that we could purchase what he called a "blanket risk-of-loss" insurance policy that would cover all of our shipments and for which we would pay the insurer based on the audited value of incoming shipments. Kay said that was the way that most companies covered themselves and that it was much less expensive than the single shipment insurance policies we were using. I am always interested in saving money, so I made a mental note to look into a policy when I returned to Nita City. No, I never told Kay that I was definitely going to make such a purchase, but I did tell him I was going to look into it.

When I got back home, I sent Mike an e-mail about the price hike. Exhibit 14 is a printout of that e-mail. I was a little surprised he didn't know about it given that it was industry wide. I also told him that there was a rumor at my gym that BMI was under investigation for antitrust violations and asked Mike to see if the price hike was related to the investigation. I also made some appointments with insurance brokers for after the first of the year to look into the blanket insurance policy. The only reason I decided to look into it myself was that I was curious about how that part of our business worked. Normally this is something Mike would handle. As far as I know, Mike was not aware that such a thing existed; not to say he didn't, but we never spoke about that kind of insurance as far as I recall.

I did speak with agents in January of YR-1 and purchased a blanket risk-of-loss policy that became effective on February 1, YR-1, and covered all of our incoming shipments. Kay was right; the policy should save us about $80,000 per year once we are fully functional. I informed Mike of the policy purchase by e-mail and reminded him to get shipment policies on incoming purchases through the end of January. Exhibit 15 is a printout of that e-mail.

By the end of YR-2, our balance sheet showed that we were only breaking even. Though we did not make any money, we didn't lose anything either, and we were very hopeful of turning a profit in YR-1. That was especially so because we got a good reaction to our base model HWCs that we sold in YR-2, and we also had an order from Neiman Marcus for 5,000 of a more sophisticated HWC in our product line to be delivered to them in April of YR-1 for inclusion in their summer catalogue. The Neiman Marcus order was important for us because it was the first sale of our more sophisticated units, which we thought would impress the market. The profit margin was relatively low on this first order ($20.00 per unit), but the prospect of a $100,000 profit was encouraging and made it likely that we would be profitable for YR-1, especially if the Neiman Marcus units were a hit and they reordered.

At any rate, the Neiman Marcus units each required three ICPs. We had only several thousand ICPs left over at the end of YR-2, so we needed the January YR-1 order from BMI that I had told Mike about in December of YR-2. The Neiman Marcus order was important to us as Neimans reached the market most inclined to be interested in our highest end (and most profitable) products. In my conversations with the Neiman Marcus buyer, Greg Smith, I was told that given the positive customer reaction he expected that they would order another 15,000 units for October YR-1 delivery; and assuming we kept up with tech developments (which was our strong suit), yearly orders in the 20,000 unit range or more were virtually assured and their typical contract was for 2 years. This was never reduced to writing because when BMI lost our parts and wouldn't replace them in time, we couldn't meet our April 1, YR-1, deadline for Neiman Marcus, and they pulled the plug on the order. Greg said he was sorry it didn't work out, but timing was everything for them, given that most of their sales of electronics were made via the Internet or through catalogues and that they needed to be able to depend on timely shipment. Just last month, in July of YR-1, Larry tried to get their business again, but he was informed by Greg Smith that they had signed a three-year exclusive for HWCs with one of our competitors, even though Smith agreed our product was superior on the technical side.

I really didn't have anything to do with the January order from BMI until February of YR-1, when I spoke with Mike about our urgent need for the platforms. He told me that there was a problem with the shipment, but Kay was working on it. I was returning from a long weekend visit with friends when I got an e-mail from Mike saying that the ICPs were lost, and that even though he had requested insurance, Kay denied that the request was made and had said the loss was our problem (Exhibit 32).

When I got back to the office, I looked over Mike's phone log, e-mail records, and letters and faxes, and agreed with him that the insurance had been requested. At Mike's suggestion I called Kay to see if I could work something out with him. Kay was very apologetic over the phone and said that he would look into replacing the shipment at no cost to us. He didn't make any promises, but he did say he would do his best for us with his legal department, that we were an important client, and that he wanted to have a long-term relationship with us. I know I also told him that we were in need of the parts to complete our Neiman Marcus order, which was very important to us. Kay said he understood, and I was optimistic that he would make the situation right and replace the ICPs, which BMI had in stock.

Because Kay was involving his lawyers, I made an appointment with our lawyer, and after talking with her, we agreed to wait and see what Kay did, given that he had promised a quick response. Kay never even gave me the courtesy of a return phone call. It was about two weeks later when I got a curt letter (Exhibit 34) that read like it was written by a lawyer, basically telling us to get lost and demanding that we pay for parts we never got. I'll admit I was angry, especially because he was so positive in our phone call and so rude not to even return the call, so I wrote him a not very nice letter (Exhibit 35). Of course, we never paid for those platforms because it was BMI's responsibility to provide us with insurance, and they failed to do so. The next we heard from BMI was when they sued us.

After I got Kay's letter in March, I immediately told Mike to get the parts from another supplier. He did—this time from Exrox. True to Kay's word, the price was 10 percent or $50,000 higher, and because of a slight difference in the configuration of the Exrox plug, we had to make a minor design change. The design change would not have been a problem if we had the parts in February, but given that BMI didn't deliver what we ordered, then screwed around in finally telling us we were out of luck, and then the design change . . . as I said, we lost the Neiman Marcus account for at least three years.

Even though as far as I can tell Mike did nothing wrong, he was down in the dumps about the problem with BMI, and for a while he was making some silly mistakes. Just to try to get him going I told him that I might have to let him go, but this was intended to jolt him out of his funk. I don't think I could ever fire Mike.

Larry is out every day trying to market our products using traditional techniques and viral marketing on the Internet. We continue to get great technical reviews and are still hoping to break into a larger market, but the Neiman Marcus opportunity was big for us, and it might be quite a while (perhaps years) before we get another good shot at the high-end market, where the real profit is. Our sales of lower-end HWCs continue, and if we do not get a bad result in this lawsuit, we should at least break even this year, maybe even make a few bucks. We would have done a hell of a lot better if BMI had done what it should have done.

DOCUMENTS AVAILABLE TO ALL SIDES

Exhibit 1

Business Machines Inc.

One Industrial Drive
Brookline, Massachusetts 02146

www.bmi.nita
Tel.: (800) BMI-2000
Fax: (877) BMI-2222

July 1, YR-2

Dear Customer,

Below are our latest prices for Integrated Chip Platforms. Please note that our price increase is the lowest in the industry. We regret the increases, but higher costs for raw materials made them impossible to avoid.

PART NO.	PRICE PER GROSS
ICP-14	$12,250.00
ICP-22	$11,500.00
ICP-26	$11,000.00
ICP-26A	$11,100.00
ICP-39	$10,800.00
ICP-40	$10,400.00
ICP-51	$ 9,250.00
ICP-52	$ 8,000.00
ICP-65	$ 7,650.00
ICP-73	$ 5,000.00
ICP-80	$ 3,850.00

NOTE:

BMI SELLS THESE PARTS IN LOTS OF ONE GROSS. SMALLER ORDERS WILL NOT BE ACCEPTED.

PAYMENT TERMS ARE CASH WITHIN SIXTY DAYS. A 2 PERCENT DISCOUNT (GOODS ONLY) IS GIVEN FOR PROMPT PAYMENT WITHIN THIRTY DAYS; 1.5 PERCENT PER MONTH IS CHARGED ON ACCOUNTS NOT PAID WITHIN SIXTY DAYS.

WE REGRET THAT WE CANNOT ACCEPT TELEPHONE OR E-MAIL ORDERS. PLEASE SEND YOUR WRITTEN ORDER BY FAX OR MAIL TO OUR NEAREST SALES OFFICE. FOR THE FAX NUMBER AND ADDRESS, CALL TOLL FREE (800) BMI-2000 OR VISIT OUR WEB SITE AT WWW.BMI.NITA.

Exhibit 2

MINICOM INC.

Outgoing Telephone Call Log

Employee: Michael Lubell

Position: VP/Purchasing

Date	Person Called	Number	Business Purpose
9/3/YR-2	Acme Café	542-2389	Ordered more cups & stirrers.
9/3/YR-2	Spring Valley Water Co.	682-9002	Ordered add'l supplies and second cooler for employee cafeteria.
9/3/YR-2	Kalo's Katering	887-5387	Ordered lunch for exec. conference.
9/3/YR-2	Houston Instruments (Mike Jenkins)	313-693-7452	Priced ICPs. None available.
9/3/YR-2	Business Machines Inc. (Chris Kay)	800-264-2000	Priced ICPs at 100g. Ordered same at 500K. They will insure at our cost.
9/3/YR-2	9AM Wire (Debbie Burnstein)	783-4636	Ordered 5K feet of CAT5 wire. Same price. They will insure at our cost.

Exhibit 3A

Sent by: Minicom Incorporated   7205555454   09/03/YR-2   11:33AM   Job 752   Page 1

Fax

To: Chris Kay

Organization: BMI

Fax: 877-BMI-2222

Phone: 800-BMI-2000

From: Michael Lubell

Date: 9/3/YR-2

Subject: ICP order

Pages: 2

Comments: The letter confirming Minicom's order is attached per our telephone conversation. A hard copy is being sent by USPS.

This facsimile is confidential and may also be privileged. If you are not the intended recipient, please notify us by telephone and either return the facsimile to us by mail or destroy it. We will reimburse you for any postage. Any use by you of the facsimile is strictly prohibited. If transmission is incomplete or if you have any questions regarding this transmission, please fax to (720) 555-5454 or call (720) 555-1212.

Exhibit 3B

Sent by: Minicom Incorporated   7205555454   09/03/YR-2   11:33AM   Job 752   Page 2

MINICOM INC.

724 Science Drive   *Phone:*   *(720) 555-1212*
Nita City, Nita 80027   *Fax:*   *(720) 555-5454*
www.minicom.biz

September 3, YR-2

VIA FAX and U.S. MAIL

Mr. Chris Kay, Sales Manager
Business Machines Incorporated
1 Industrial Drive
Brookline, MA 02146

Dear Mr. Kay:

This is to confirm our phone conversation earlier today in which we agreed to the following transaction. Business Machines Incorporated agrees to sell 100 gross of ICPs (your part no. ICP-73) at $5,000 per gross for a total price of $500,000. Shipment will be made within ten days to our offices via National Parcel Service, and BMI will insure the shipment for full value.

Minicom Incorporated agrees to pay the total purchase price plus shipping and insurance charges. Payment within thirty days after receipt of goods will be credited with a 2 percent discount. Payment between thirty and sixty days after receipt will be for the full price. Payment after sixty days will include a 1.5 percent per month finance charge.

Please notify me if this letter does not conform to your understanding of our agreement.

Yours truly,

Michael Lubell
Vice President Purchasing
michael@minicom.biz

ML/jaf

Exhibit 3C

724 Science Drive	*Phone:*	*(720) 555-1212*
Nita City, Nita 80027	*Fax:*	*(720) 555-5454*
www.minicom.biz		

September 3, YR-2

VIA FAX and U.S. MAIL

Mr. Chris Kay, Sales Manager
Business Machines Incorporated
1 Industrial Drive
Brookline, MA 02146

Dear Mr. Kay:

This is to confirm our phone conversation earlier today in which we agreed to the following transaction. Business Machines Incorporated agrees to sell 100 gross of ICPs (your part no. ICP-73) at $5,000 per gross for a total price of $500,000. Shipment will be made within ten days to our offices via National Parcel Service, and BMI will insure the shipment for full value.

Minicom Incorporated agrees to pay the total purchase price plus shipping and insurance charges. Payment within thirty days after receipt of goods will be credited with a 2 percent discount. Payment between thirty and sixty days after receipt will be for the full price. Payment after sixty days will include a 1.5 percent per month finance charge.

Please notify me if this letter does not conform to your understanding of our agreement.

Yours truly,

Michael Lubell

Michael Lubell
Vice President Purchasing
michael@minicom.biz

ML/jaf

RECEIVED

SEPT 06 YR-2

Exhibit 4

From: virginiayoung.2@bmi.nita
Reply-to: order_confirm@bmi.nita

To: shipping22@bmi.nita

Subject: Work order

Date: Fri, 6 Sep YR-2 13:29:34-0500 (EDT)

Order confirmed today requires shipment immediately of 100 gross of ICP-73 to

Minicom Inc.
724 Science Drive
Nita City, Nita 80027

Ship NPS prepaid insure for 500,000.

Shipment Date: 9-6-YR-2

Warehouseman: Tim Groody

ATTACHMENTS\:

Exhibit 5

NATIONAL PARCEL SERVICE

SHIPPING RECORD

SHIPPING RECEIPT—WHITE
NPS COPY—CANARY

RECEIVED FROM

NAME:	Business Machines Inc.	DATE:	9/6/YR-2
STREET:	One Industrial Drive		
CITY/STATE:	Brookline, Mass.	ZIP CODE:	02146

SEND TO

NAME:	MINICOM Inc.		
STREET:	724 Science Drive		
CITY/STATE:	Nita City, Nita	ZIP CODE:	80027

IF COD	DECLARED VALUE	ZONE	
		AIR	GROUND
$ _____	$ _____		STD
AMOUNT	AMOUNT		

PACKAGE CONTENTS

25 GROSS ICP-73

DO NOT WRITE BELOW THIS LINE

TYPE CHARGE	CUSTOMER COUNTER	DATE	TRAN	CHARGES AMOUNT
COD _____	$125,000		Insurance:	$ 277.50
			Shipping	30.65
EXCESS VALUTATION _____				$ 308.15
PACKAGE _____	210			

Unless a greater value is declared in writing on this receipt, the shipper hereby declares and agrees that the released value of each package or article not enclosed in a package covered by this receipt is $100, which is a reasonable value under the circumstances surrounding the transportation. The entry of a DOC amount is not a declaration of value. In addition, the maximum value for an air service shipment is $5,000 and the maximum carrier liability is $5,000. Claims not made to carrier within nine months of shipment date are waived. Customer's check accepted at shipper's risk unless otherwise noted on COD tag.

Thank you for using NATIONAL PARCEL SERVICE

NOTE: Three more of the above receipts appear in the records of BMI and were produced. They are identical in every respect to the one shown above.

Exhibit 6

Business Machines Inc.

One Industrial Drive
Brookline, Massachusetts 02146

www.bmi.nita
Tel.: (800) BMI-2000
Fax: (877) BMI-2222

September 16, YR-2

Mr. Michael Lubell
Minicom Incorporated
724 Science Drive
Nita City, NI 80027

Dear Mr. Lubell:

Thank you for your recent first order from Business Machines Incorporated. We hope your purchase represents the beginning of a long and successful business relationship.

As noted in the attached statement of account, we have shipped your goods as per our agreement. Please notify me immediately if the goods are in any way unsatisfactory or if any error appears in your statement.

BMI appreciates your business.

Sincerely,

Chris Kay

Chris Kay
Sales Manager
Eastern Subdivision II
chris.kay@bmi.nita

CK/vy

Encl.

RECEIVED

09 19 YR-2

Exhibit 7

Business Machines Inc.

One Industrial Drive
Brookline, Massachusetts 02146

www.bmi.nita
Tel.: (800) BMI-2000
Fax: (877) BMI-2222

STATEMENT OF ACCOUNT

September 16, YR-2

Minicom Inc.
724 Science Drive
Nita City, NI 80027
Attn: Mr. Michael Lubell

Date	Items Shipped	Debit	Credit
9/16/YR-2	100 Gross ICP-73	$ 500,000.00	
	Shipping	122.60	
	Insurance	1,110.00	
BALANCE DUE			
		$ 501,232.60	

Accounts paid within thirty days receive a 2 percent discount (goods only) for prompt payment. Full payment is due within sixty days. Interest of 1.5 percent per month will be added to accounts after sixty days.

Exhibit 8

724 Science Drive   *Phone:* *(720) 555-1212*
Nita City, Nita 80027   *Fax:* *(720) 555-5454*
www.minicom.biz

September 23, YR-2

Mr. Chris Kay, Sales Manager
Business Machines Incorporated
1 Industrial Drive
Brookline, MA 02146

Dear Mr. Kay:

Thank you for your prompt shipment of ICP-73s. They were received in good order. Enclosed please find our check #2104 in the amount of $491,232.60 representing the purchase price plus shipping and insurance, less the 2 percent ($10,000.00) discount for prompt payment. We look forward to conducting business with you on this basis in the future.

Yours truly,

Michael Lubell

Michael Lubell
Vice President Purchasing
michael@minicom.biz

ML/jaf

Encl.

RECEIVED

SEPT 26 YR-2

Exhibit 9

MINICOM INC.	2104

724 Science Drive
Nita City, Nita 80027
Phone (720) 555-1212

September 23, YR-2

PAY TO THE ORDER OF:

Business Machines Incorporated $ 491,232.60

Four hundred ninety-one thousand two hundred thirty-two and 60/100   DOLLARS

Nita National Bank
Nita City, Nita 80027

Elliot Milstein

Memo_____

ENDORSE CHECK HERE:

PAY TO THE ORDER OF
Business Machines Inc.
NITA NATIONAL BANK
Nita City, Nita 80027
FOR DEPOSIT ONLY
September 30th, Yr-2

Exhibit 10

MINICOM INC.

Incoming Telephone Call Log

Employee: Elliot Milstein

Position: President

Date	Person Called	Business Purpose
11/12/YR-2	Crot, Watershed Accounting	Discussed preparation for year-end audit.
11/12/YR-2	Edward Austin Buyer, Staples	Discussed our new HANDe. Referred call to Larry Schwartz, VP for Sales.
11/12/YR-2	Chris Kay	I accepted Expo invite. He will send a formal invitation.
11/12/YR-2	Joe Kalo	Wants payment for last executive lunch. Referred to Silver, VP Accounting.
11/12/YR-2	Greg Smith	Neiman Marcus follow-up from Larry – Agreed to ship 5,000 units of ACC model HWC by 4/1/YR-1 at $180.00/unit/ 10/1 – 15 k units if quality OK

Exhibit 11

Business Machines Incorporated

Requests the pleasure of your company at our

Eastern Regional Exposition of Computer Products

at

The Inn Hilton Head, South Carolina

from Thursday, December 12

through Sunday, December 15, YR-2

R. S. V. P. (800) BMI-2000

RECEIVED
11 12 YR-2

Exhibit 12

Business Machines Inc.

One Industrial Drive
Brookline, Massachusetts 02146

www.bmi.nita
Tel.: (800) BMI-2000
Fax: (877) BMI-2222

November 18, YR-2

Mr. Elliot Milstein, President
Minicom Inc.
724 Science Drive
Nita City, NI 80027

Dear Elliot:

I am delighted you and your wife will be able to join us at Hilton Head. Because of the business purpose of the Expo, BMI will, of course, pay all expenses for you and your wife, including air fare. I have taken the liberty of reserving a one-bedroom suite on the golf course for you.

I look forward to seeing you at the Expo and on the golf course.

Best regards,

Chris Kay
Sales Manager
Eastern Subdivision II
chris.kay@bmi.nita

CK/vy

P.S. Please notify my assistant, Virginia Young, of both your golf handicaps so we may properly pair you for the tournament.

**RECEIVED
11 22 YR-2**

Exhibit 13

MINICOM INC.

Outgoing Telephone Call Log

Employee: Elliot Milstein

Position: President

Date	Person Called	Number	Business Purpose
12/13/YR-2	Crot Watershed Accounting	429-3417	Check status of year-end audit.
12/13/YR-2	Voyager Ins. Co.	427-1420	Asked about risk-of-loss insurance. They do not offer.
12/13/YR-2	Vermont General Ins. Co.	802-529-2178	R of L policy not available. Try New Britain L & C.
12/13/YR-2	New Britain Life & Casualty	203-765-2257	They offer policy. Flat premium covers up to $50,000/shipment.
12/13/YR-2	Skipper Ins. Co.	422-1925	Same policy will run less than NBL & C. Agent to make appt. to come in after 1st of year.
12/13/YR-2	Kalo's Katering	887-5397	Discussed service at the last exec. lunch. Promises prompt delivery next time.
12/13/YR-2	Neiman Marcus (Greg Smith)	214-323-5974	Confirmed order of 5,000 units HWCs to be delivered no later than April 1, YR-1

Exhibit 14

From:	elliot@minicom.biz
Reply to:	<none>
To:	michael@minicom.biz

Subject:	Purchase of ICPs
Date:	Sun., 15 Dec YR-2 16:48:22 -700 (MST)
cc:	
bcc:	Attachments\: <none>

Before you leave for vacation, I wanted to remind you that we need to place an order for ICPs with BMI for Neiman 5k unit order for April 1 — 15k potential order on 10/1. The accountants tell me that our cash flow situation will be better after the first of the year, so I suggest that you wait until early January to place the order.

Chris Kay of BMI told me recently that there is an industry-wide price increase of 10 percent coming on March 1. The word at the club is that BMI is in some kind of antitrust trouble with the Justice Department in Washington. You might try to subtly find out if they still plan to go ahead with the price hike.

Exhibit 15

From:	elliot@minicom.biz
Reply to:	\<none\>
To:	michael@minicom.biz

Subject:	Insurance on Purchases/Change in Policy
Date:	Fri, 3 Jan YR-1 11:25:10 -0700 (MST)
cc:	
bcc:	Attachments\\: \<none\>

This is to let you know that today I purchased what is called a blanket risk-of-loss insurance policy to cover all incoming shipments. The purchase was from the Skipper Insurance Company. The policy goes into effect on February 1 of this year. We should continue to follow our standard procedure of insuring all incoming shipments individually until that date. After February 1, all purchases will be insured automatically.

Mike, this is a tip I picked up at Hilton Head. It should save us about $80,000 a year. Looks like this business may make it after all.

Exhibit 16

From:	michael@minicom.biz
Reply to:	<none>
To:	chris.kay@bmi.nita

Subject:	ICP-73 order
Date:	Fri., 3 Jan YR-1 13:15:44 -0700 (MST)
cc:	
bcc:	Attachments\: <none>

Mr Kay,

Please advise on the availability of 100 gross ICP-73 at $5,000 per gross on the same payment and shipping conditions as our September YR-2 order.

Michael

Michael Lubell, VP Purchasing
Minicom, Inc.
www.minicom.biz

Exhibit 17

From:	virginiayoung.2@bmi.nita
Reply-to:	order_confirm@bmi.nita
To:	michael@minicom.biz

Subject:	Your inquiry
Date:	Fri., 3 Jan YR-1 16:58:16 -0500 (EST)

Mr. Lubell,

Thank you for your interest in placing an order with us. We have 100 gross ICP-73 in stock for immediate shipment. Price is $500,000 for 100 gross. Payment terms remain same per our price list. Please place your order via fax or mail.

Virginia Young
BMI
One Industrial Drive
Brookline, MA 02416
(800) BMI-2000

ATTACHMENTS\:

Exhibit 18

MINICOM INC.

Outgoing Telephone Call Log

Employee: Michael Lubell

Position: VP/Purchasing

Date	Person Called	Number	Business Purpose
1/6/YR-1	Kalo's Katering	887-5387	Ordered exec. lunch for today.
1/6/YR-1	Information Officer Justice Dept. Antitrust Div.	202-421-3000	Inquired about BMI antitrust problems. Details not available to public, but officer seemed to know about it.
1/6/YR-1	BMI Chris Kay	800-264-2000	Ordered 100g ICP-73 at $5,000/g. They will insure at our cost. I will confirm by letter.
1/6/YR-1	Opp's Plumbing	347-2281	Will come 6:30 A.M. tomorrow to repair exec. toilet. Night watchman to be notified.

Exhibit 19

From:	virginiayoung.2@bmi.nita
Reply-to:	
To:	chris.kay@bmi.nita

Subject:	message
Date:	Mon., 6 Jan YR-1 11:15:26 -0500 (EST)

Michael Lubell of Minicom Inc. telephoned about a potential order and would like you to return his call at (720) 555-1212.

ATTACHMENTS\:

Exhibit 20A

Sent by: Minicom Incorporated   7205555454   01/06/YR-1   11:46AM   Job 527   Page 1

FAX

Name: Chris Kay

Organization: BMI

Fax: 877-BMI-2222

Phone: 800-BMI-2000

From: Michael Lubell

Date: 1/6/YR-1

Subject: ICP order

Pages: 2

Comments: The letter confirming Minicom's phone order is attached. A hard copy is being sent by USPS.

This facsimile is confidential and may also be privileged. If you are not the intended recipient, please notify us by telephone and either return the facsimile to us by mail or destroy it. We will reimburse you for any postage. Any use by you of the facsimile is strictly prohibited. If transmission is incomplete or if you have any questions regarding this transmission, please fax to (720) 555-5454 or call (720) 555-1212.

Exhibit 20B

Sent by: Minicom Incorporated   7205555454   01/06/YR-1   11:46AM   Job527   Page 2

MINICOM INC.

724 Science Drive   *Phone:* *(720) 555-1212*
Nita City, Nita 80027   *Fax:*   *(720) 555-5454*

www.minicom.biz

January 6, YR-1

SENT VIA FAX

Mr. Chris Kay
Business Machines Incorporated
1 Industrial Drive
Brookline, MA 02146

Dear Mr. Kay:

This is to confirm my call earlier today with your administrative assistant. We have placed an order for 100 gross of ICP-73s at $5,000 per gross for a total price of $500,000. It is my understanding that the transaction will be handled as per the usual agreement. Please notify me immediately if this letter does not conform to your understanding of our agreement.

Yours truly,

Michael Lubell
Vice President Purchasing
michael@minicom.biz

ML/jaf

Exhibit 20C

724 Science Drive   *Phone:* *(720) 555-1212*
Nita City, Nita 80027   *Fax:*   *(720) 555-5454*

www.minicom.biz

January 6, YR-1

Mr. Chris Kay
Business Machines Incorporated
1 Industrial Drive
Brookline, MA 02146

Dear Mr. Kay:

This is to confirm my call earlier today with your administrative assistant. We have placed an order for 100 gross of ICP-73s at $5,000 per gross for a total price of $500,000. It is my understanding that the transaction will be handled as per the usual agreement. Please notify me immediately if this letter does not conform to your understanding of our agreement.

Yours truly,

Michael Lubell

Michael Lubell
Vice President Purchasing
michael@minicom.biz

ML/jaf

RECEIVED

JAN 10 YR-1

Exhibit 21

From:	virginiayoung.2@bmi.nita
Reply-to:	order_confirm@bmi.nita
To:	shipping22@bmi.nita

Subject:	Work order
Date:	Fri., 10 Jan YR-1 :12:55 -0500 (EST)

Order confirmed today requires shipment immediately of 100 gross of ICP-73 to

Minicom Inc.
724 Science Drive
Nita City, Nita 80027

Ship NPS.
Shipment Date: 1-17-YR-1
Warehouseman: Tim Groody

ATTACHMENTS\:

Exhibit 22

Business Machines Inc.

One Industrial Drive
Brookline, Massachusetts 02146

www.bmi.nita
Tel.: (800) BMI-2000
Fax: (877) BMI-2222

January 10, YR-1

Mr. Michael Lubell
Minicom Incorporated
724 Science Drive
Nita City, NI 80027

Dear Mr. Lubell:

Thank you for your recent order from Business Machines Incorporated. As noted in the attached statement of account, we have shipped your order as per our agreement. Please notify me immediately if the goods are in any way unsatisfactory or if any error appears in your statement.

BMI appreciates your business.

Sincerely,

Chris Kay /vey

Chris Kay
Sales Manager
Eastern Subdivision II
chris.kay@bmi.nita

CK/vy

Encl.

RECEIVED
01 13 YR-1

Exhibit 23

Business Machines Inc.

One Industrial Drive
Brookline, Massachusetts 02146

www.bmi.nita
Tel.: (800) BMI-2000
Fax: (877) BMI-2222

STATEMENT OF ACCOUNT

January 10, YR-1

Minicom Inc.
724 Science Drive
Nita City, NI 80027
Attn: Mr. Michael Lubell

Date	Items Shipped	Debit	Credit
9/6/YR-2		$ 500,000.00	
	Shipping	$ 122.60	
	Insurance	$ 1,110.00	
		$ 501,232.60	
9/25/YR-2	Payment received		$ 491,232.60
	2% credit for		
	prompt payment		$ 10,000.00
BALANCE DUE		**-0-**	
1/10/YR-1	100 Gross ICP- 73	$ 500,000.00	
	Shipping	$ 122.60	
BALANCE DUE		**$ 500,122.60**	

Accounts paid within thirty days receive a 2 percent discount (goods only) for prompt payment. Full payment is due within sixty days. Interest of 1.5 percent per month will be added to accounts after sixty days.

RECEIVED
01 13 YR-1

Exhibit 24

NATIONAL
PARCEL SERVICE

SHIPPING RECORD

SHIPPING RECEIPT—WHITE
NPS COPY—CANARY

RECEIVED FROM

NAME:	Business Machines Inc.	DATE:	1/17/YR-1
STREET:	One Industrial Drive		
CITY/STATE:	Brookline, Mass.	ZIP CODE:	02146

SEND TO

NAME:	MINICOM Inc.		
STREET:	724 Science Drive		
CITY/STATE:	Nita City, Nita	ZIP CODE:	80027

IF COD	DECLARED VALUE	ZONE	
$ _____	$ _____	AIR	GROUND
AMOUNT	AMOUNT		STD

PACKAGE CONTENTS

25 GROSS ICP-73

DO NOT WRITE BELOW THIS LINE

TYPE CHARGE	CUSTOMER COUNTER	DATE	TRAN	CHARGES AMOUNT
COD				
_____				
EXCESS				
_____				
VALUTATION				
_____				
PACKAGE				
_____	210			$ 30.65

Unless a greater value is declared in writing on this receipt, the shipper hereby declares and agrees that the released value of each package or article not enclosed in a package covered by this receipt is $100, which is a reasonable value under the circumstances surrounding the transportation. The entry of a DOC amount is not a declaration of value. In addition, the maximum value for an air service shipment is $5,000 and the maximum carrier liability is $5,000. Claims not made to carrier within nine months of shipment date are waived. Customer's check accepted at shipper's risk unless otherwise noted on COD tag.

NOTE: Three more of the above receipts appear in the records of BMI and were produced. They are identical in every respect to the one shown above.

Exhibit 25

NPS

NATIONAL
PARCEL SERVICE

SHIPPING RECORD

SHIPPING RECEIPT—WHITE
NPS COPY—CANARY

RECEIVED FROM

NAME:	Business Machines Inc.	DATE:	1/17/YR-1
STREET:	One Industrial Drive		
CITY/STATE:	Brookline, Mass.	ZIP CODE:	02146

SEND TO

NAME:	MINICOM Inc.		
STREET:	724 Science Drive		
CITY/STATE:	Nita City, Nita	ZIP CODE:	80027

IF COD	DECLARED VALUE	ZONE	
$ _____	$ _____	AIR	GROUND
AMOUNT	AMOUNT		STD

PACKAGE CONTENTS

10 GROSS ICP-73

DO NOT WRITE BELOW THIS LINE

TYPE CHARGE	CUSTOMER COUNTER	DATE	TRAN	CHARGES AMOUNT
COD				
_____				
EXCESS				
_____				
VALUTATION				
_____				
PACKAGE				
_____	210			$ 30.65

Unless a greater value is declared in writing on this receipt, the shipper hereby declares and agrees that the released value of each package or article not enclosed in a package covered by this receipt is $100, which is a reasonable value under the circumstances surrounding the transportation. The entry of a DOC amount is not a declaration of value. In addition, the maximum value for an air service shipment is $5,000 and the maximum carrier liability is $5,000. Claims not made to carrier within nine months of shipment date are waived. Customer's check accepted at shipper's risk unless otherwise noted on COD tag.

NOTE: Three more of the above receipts appear in the records of BMI and were produced. They are identical in every respect to the one shown above.

Exhibit 26

NPS

*NATIONAL PARCEL
SERVICE*

SHIPPING RECORD

SHIPPING RECEIPT—WHITE
NPS COPY—CANARY

RECEIVED FROM

NAME:	MINICOM Inc.	DATE:	1/24/YR-1
STREET:	724 Science Drive		
CITY/STATE:	Nita City, Nita	ZIP CODE:	80027

SEND TO

NAME:	Business Machines Inc.		
STREET:	One Industrial Drive		
CITY/STATE:	Brookline, Mass.	ZIP CODE:	02146

IF COD	DECLARED VALUE	ZONE	
$ _____	$ _____	AIR	GROUND
AMOUNT	AMOUNT		STD

PACKAGE CONTENTS

10 GROSS ICP-22

DO NOT WRITE BELOW THIS LINE

TYPE CHARGE	CUSTOMER COUNTER	DATE	TRAN	CHARGES AMOUNT
COD				
_____	$115,000		Insurance:	$ 270.50
			Shipping	30.25
EXCESS VALUTATION				$ 300.15
PACKAGE				
_____	210			

Unless a greater value is declared in writing on this receipt, the shipper hereby declares and agrees that the released value of each package or article not enclosed in a package covered by this receipt is $100, which is a reasonable value under the circumstances surrounding the transportation. The entry of a DOC amount is not a declaration of value. In addition, the maximum value for an air service shipment is $5,000 and the maximum carrier liability is $5,000. Claims not made to carrier within nine months of shipment date are waived. Customer's check accepted at shipper's risk unless otherwise noted on COD tag.

Thank you for using NATIONAL PARCEL SERVICE

NOTE: Three more of the above receipts appear in the records of BMI and were produced. They are identical in every respect to the one shown above.

Exhibit 27

724 Science Drive   *Phone:*   *(720) 555-1212*
Nita City, Nita 80027   *Fax:*   *(720) 555-5454*

www.minicom.biz

January 24, YR-1

Mr. Chris Kay
Business Machines Incorporated
1 Industrial Drive
Brookline, MA 02146

Dear Mr. Kay:

We received today a shipment of 40 gross of ICP-22s from your Eastern Warehouse No. 22 mislabeled as ICP-73. As your records should reflect, our order was for <u>100</u> gross of ICP-73s. We have today returned the incorrect shipment. Shipping and insurance for the return comes to $300.75. Please remit this amount at your earliest convenience.

In reviewing your bill of 1/10/YR-1, I have noted that you failed to charge us for insurance on your last shipment. Please make the necessary correction.

Our Vice President for Production informs me that we will need the parts by January 31, YR-1, for a large April 1 order. Please advise me immediately as to when we can expect delivery.

Thank you for your prompt attention to this matter.

Yours truly,

Michael Lubell

Michael Lubell
Vice President Purchasing
michael@minicom.biz

ML/jaf

**RECEIVED
JAN 27 YR-1**

Exhibit 28

Business Machines Inc.

One Industrial Drive
Brookline, Massachusetts 02146

www.bmi.nita
Tel.: (800) BMI-2000
Fax: (877) BMI-2222

January 27, YR-1

Mr. Michael Lubell
Minicom Inc.
724 Science Drive
Nita City, NI 80027

Dear Mr. Lubell:

Thank you for the return of the goods erroneously sent to you by Business Machines Incorporated. Your account will be credited for the full amount of shipping and insurance charges for the return. As we have risk-of-loss insurance, in the unlikely event this situation occurs again, there is no need for you to insure any shipment of goods to BMI.

Our records indicate that the shipment of 100 gross of ICP-73s was sent via NPS prepaid on 1/17/YR-1. We have contacted NPS, and they are tracing the shipment. We apologize for any delay caused by their error.

I expect you will receive your order in the very near future. BMI appreciates your business.

Sincerely,

Chris Kay

Chris Kay
Sales Manager
Eastern Subdivision II
chris.kay@bmi.nita

CK/vy

**RECEIVED
01 31 YR-1**

Exhibit 29

Business Machines Inc.

One Industrial Drive
Brookline, Massachusetts 02146

www.bmi.nita
Tel.: (800) BMI-2000
Fax: (877) BMI-2222

February 14, YR-1

Mr. Michael Lubell
Minicom Inc.
24 Science Drive
Nita City, NI 80027

Dear Mr. Lubell:

I have finally heard from NPS regarding your missing shipment. After much prodding, they finally admitted that the shipment was lost by them. Their check for $400.00, the full amount of their admitted liability, is enclosed. As you will note, I have endorsed it over to you. Should you wish to discuss this matter with NPS, their Claims Manager is Sharon Cupitt.

We have replenished our supply of ICP-73s and stand ready to fill any future orders at our current prices. However, as I informed Elliot at Hilton Head, our prices will go up 10 percent on March 1.

BMI appreciates your business.

Sincerely,

Chris Kay

Chris Kay
Sales Manager
Eastern Subdivision II
chris.kay@bmi.nita

CK/vy

Encl.

RECEIVED
02 18 YR-1

Exhibit 30

≡NPS≡	**0225**
NATIONAL PARCEL SERVICE	February 11, YR-1

PAY TO THE ORDER OF:

Business Machines Inc. $ 400.00

Four hundred and no/100   DOLLARS

Sharon Cupitt

NATIONAL PARCEL SERVICE

**THE CITIZENS & SOUTHERN
NATIONAL BANK
SAVANNAH, GEORGIA**

*Pay to the order of
Minicom
Thal. Ross
Asst. Cntllr.*

Exhibit 31

MINICOM INC.

Outgoing Telephone Call Log

Employee: Michael Lubell

Position: VP/Purchasing

Date	Person Called	Number	Business Purpose
2/21/YR-1	NPS Sharon Cupitt	428-3134	NPS liability w/o insurance is $100 per package.
2/21/YR-1	BMI Chris Kay	800-264-2000	Called re: lost order. Kay says it's our problem. Says we didn't request insurance.
2/21/YR-1	Kalo's Katering	887-5397	Changed sandwiches from pastrami to turkey for exec. lunch.
2/21/YR-1	Opp's Plumbing	347-2281	Told them that bill will not be paid until toilet is properly fixed.
2/21/YR-1	Brown's Body Shop	389-2187	Wife's car will cost $825 for repairs.
2/21/YR-1	Potter's Pharmacy	273-4189	Ordered refill on Paxil. Generic now available. Will be ready at 5 p.m.

Exhibit 32

From:	michael@minicom.biz
Reply to:	\<none\>
To:	elliot@minicom.biz

Subject:	BMI shipment
date:	Fri., 21 Feb YR-1 14:13:09 -0700 (MST)
cc:	
bcc:	Attachments\: \<none\>

As I mentioned several days ago, we are having trouble with our shipment of ICP-73s from BMI. Enclosed is a copy of a letter from Chris Kay, which indicates that they will not assume any liability. I checked with him by phone and that is the position they are taking. He says that in the absence of a specific request they do not insure and he received no word from his administrative assistant that I requested insurance. He also says that my confirming letter, which clearly states the transaction was to be on the same terms as the last when they did insure, was not understood that way by him. My phone log, by the way, does indicate his assistant was told to get insurance on the shipment for its full value and agreed to the same.

I know you have a personal relationship with Kay, and I suggest you contact him directly. I do not believe I can accomplish anything further on this matter. NPS, of course, takes the position that their liability in the absence of insurance is limited to $100 per package for a total of $400. We have a check for that amount, which we have not deposited.

Exhibit 33

MINICOM INC.

Outgoing Telephone Call Log

Employee: Elliot Milstein

Position: President

Date	Person Called	Number	Business Purpose
2/21/YR-1	Chris Kay	800-264-2000	Will check out problem with legal dept. and write ASAP.
2/21/YR-1	Horton, Stein & Benson	343-2180	Made appt. for 2/25 at Kalo's Kitchen for lunch meeting.

Exhibit 34

Business Machines Inc.

One Industrial Drive
Brookline, Massachusetts 02146

www.bmi.nita
Tel.: (800) BMI-2000
Fax: (877) BMI-2222

March 3, YR-1

Mr. Elliot Milstein
Minicom Inc.
724 Science Drive
Nita City, NI 80027

Dear Mr. Milstein:

I have reviewed with our legal department the status of our recent transaction. Under the terms of our contract, as controlled by the Uniform Commercial Code, the risk of loss of this shipment clearly falls upon your company. We regret to inform you that we cannot be responsible for the losses your company has incurred and must instead demand that you make payment of the amounts due BMI as shown in our previous billing to you.

I am informed that all subsequent correspondence about this matter should be referred to Mr. John W. Davis in our General Counsel's office.

Sincerely,

Chris Kay
Sales Manager
Eastern Subdivision II
chris.kay@bmi.nita

CK/vy

Encl.

cc: John W. Davis

**RECEIVED
MAR 07 YR-1**

Exhibit 35

724 Science Drive   Phone: (720) 555-1212
Nita City, Nita 80027   Fax: (720) 555-5454
www.minicom.biz

March 7, YR-1

Mr. Chris Kay
Business Machines Incorporated
Industrial Drive
Brookline, MA 02146

Dear Mr. Kay:

When we met in Hilton Head last December, you assured me that in dealing with Business Machines Incorporated I would find your company to be concerned with the success of my business. As you know, we are a young company and cannot afford substantial losses that are avoidable, so we take every precaution necessary to safeguard our working capital. When we ordered the ICP-73s from your company in September, we requested that you send them insured and you did. We made the same request at the time of the January order. This time BMI did not comply, and your failure, you claim, should cost us $500,000 plus the $50,000 price increase that has gone into effect since our first order.

If anyone deserves to bear this cost, it is BMI. Our company did everything possible to avoid the loss; BMI failed to do anything to help us in this regard. Contrary to the language of your company's slogan, "BMI appreciates your business," it looks to me that the correct statement is "BMI gives you the business."

I have referred this matter to our attorney, and you will be hearing from him in the future.

Sincerely,

Elliot Milstein

Elliot Milstein
President
elliot@minicom.biz

EM/jaf

cc: Charles A. Horton

RECEIVED
03 10 YR-1

Exhibit 36

MINICOM INC.

Outgoing Telephone Call Log

Employee: Michael Lubell

Position: VP/Purchasing

Date	Person Called	Number	Business Purpose
3/10/YR-1	Gold's Delicatessen	381-4262	Ordered exec. lunch.
3/10/YR-1	Exrox Inc. Brent Taylor	617-429-3800	Ordered 100g MICP-2 (same as ICP-73). Ship NPS. 550K.
3/10/YR-1	Computer Innovations Les Ottolenghi	387-2188	Asked about sales openings. Sent resume.
3/10/YR-1	Dell Corp.	394-5087	Ditto

Exhibit 37

From:	michael@minicom.biz
Reply to:	<none>
To:	btaylor@exrox.nita

Subject:	Order
Date:	Mon, 10 Mar YR-1 11:07:10 -0700 (MST)
cc:	
bcc:	Attachments\: <none>

Mr. Taylor,

This is to confirm our phone conversation earlier today, in which we agreed to the following transaction. Exrox agrees to sell 100 gross of Integrated Chip Platforms (your part number MICP-2) at $5,500.00 per gross for a total price of $550,000. Minicom may pay the full price within 30 days of receipt and receive a 2% discount for prompt payment. Payment after 30 days, but before 60 days, will be at full price. Payment after 60 days will include 1% per month finance charge. Exrox agrees to ship via NPS. Minicom agrees to pay all shipping costs.

Please notify me immediately if the above does not adequately reflect our agreement.

Michael

Michael Lubell, VP Purchasing
Minicom, Inc.
www.minicom.biz

Exhibit 38

 ®

One Computer Drive
Brookline, Massachusetts 02146

Tel.: (617) 429-3800
Fax: (617) 429-2900

March 14, YR-1

Mr. Michael Lubell
Minicom Incorporated
724 Science Drive
Nita City, NI 80027

Dear Mr. Lubell:

Thank you for your recent order, which has been shipped today. Please let me know if the merchandise is satisfactory.

Your statement is enclosed.

Sincerely,

Brent A. Taylor

Brent A. Taylor
Sales Manager
Microcomputer Parts

BT/pam

Encl.

RECEIVED
03 18 YR-1

Exhibit 39

One Computer Drive
Brookline, Massachusetts 02146

Tel.: (617) 429-3800
Fax: (617) 429-2900

March 14, YR-1

STATEMENT OF ACCOUNT

Minicom Inc.
724 Science Drive
Nita City, Nita 80027

Date	Goods Shipped	Price	Payment	Balance Due
3/14/YR-1	100 gross MICP-2	$ 550,00.00		
	Ship via NPS	140.60		
				$ 550,140.60

Interest will be charged on accounts after sixty days at the rate of 1 percent/month or part thereof.

RECEIVED
03 18 YR-1

Exhibit 40

From:	elliot@minicom.biz
Reply to:	\<none\>
To:	gsmith@neimanmarcus.nita

Subject:	HWC Order
Date:	27 Mar YR-1 09:30:10 -0700 (MST)
CC:	
BCC:	Attachments\: \<none\>

Greg:

We have encountered a supplier problem and will not be able to make the April 1 deadline for the HWCs—can you give me a couple extra weeks? The product will be first rate.

Exhibit 41

From:	gsmith@neimanmarcus.nita
Reply to:	\<none\>
To:	elliot@minicom.biz

Subject:	Re: HWC Order
Date:	27 Mar YR-1 16:30:10 -0700 (MST)
CC:	
BCC:	Attachments\: \<none\>

Elliot

I am so sorry I cannot accommodate you. Had to call other bidder on contract. They can provide immediately—my superiors insist on going with the sure thing. Hope we can do some business in the future, but we are out for now.

Sorry again.

Greg

Exhibit 42

 ®

One Computer Drive
Brookline, Massachusetts 02146

Tel.: (617) 429-3800
Fax: (617) 429-2900

June 13, YR-1

STATEMENT OF ACCOUNT

Minicom Inc.
724 Science Drive
Nita City, NI 80027

Date	Goods Shipped	Price	Payment	Balance Due
3/14/YR-1	100 gross MICP-2	$ 550,000.00		
	Ship via NPS	$ 140.60		
				$ 550,140.60
6/13/YR-1	Interest	$ 5,500.00		**$ 5,500.00**
			Balance Now Due	**$ 555,640.60**

**RECEIVED
06 16 YR-1**

Exhibit 43

724 Science Drive   *Phone:* *(720) 555-1212*
Nita City, Nita 80027   *Fax:*   *(720) 555-5454*

www.minicom.biz

June 20, YR-1

Mr. Brent Taylor

EXROX Incorporated
1 Computer Drive
Brookline, MA 02146

Dear Mr. Taylor:

Thank you for your recent delivery of MICP-2 Integrated Chip Platforms. We apologize for our delay in payment, which was a result of differences with a former supplier. Our check for the purchase price plus interest is enclosed.

We look forward to doing business with you in the future. Yours truly,

Michael Lubell
Vice President Purchasing
michael@minicom.biz

ML/jaf

Encl.

COPY

Exhibit 44

MINICOM INC.	**2115**
724 Science Drive	
Nita City, Nita 80027	
Phone (720) 555-1212	June 20 YR-1

PAY TO THE ORDER OF:

Exrox Incorporated $ 555,640.60

Five hundred fifty-five thousand six hundred forty and 60/100   DOLLARS

Nita National Bank
Nita City, Nita 80027   *Elliot Wilstein*

*Memo*_____

ENDORSE CHECK HERE:

PAY TO THE ORDER OF
Exrox Incorporated
NITA NATIONAL BANK
Nita City, Nita 80027
FOR DEPOSIT ONLY

General Jury Instructions

Nita Instruction 01:01—Introduction

You have been selected as jurors and have taken an oath to well and truly try this cause. This trial will last one day.

During the progress of the trial there will be periods of time when the Court recesses. During those periods of time, you must not talk about this case among yourselves or with anyone else.

During the trial, do not talk to any of the parties, their lawyers, or any of the witnesses.

If any attempt is made by anyone to talk to you concerning the matters here under consideration, you should immediately report that fact to the Court.

You should keep an open mind. You should not form or express an opinion during the trial and should reach no conclusion in this case until you have heard all of the evidence, the arguments of counsel, and the final instructions as to the law that will be given to you by the Court.

Nita Instruction 01:02—Conduct of the Trial

First, the attorneys will have an opportunity to make opening statements. These statements are not evidence and should be considered only as a preview of what the attorneys expect the evidence will be.

Following the opening statements, witnesses will be called to testify. They will be placed under oath and questioned by the attorneys. Documents and other tangible exhibits may also be received as evidence. If an exhibit is given to you to examine, you should examine it carefully, individually, and without any comment.

It is counsel's right and duty to object when testimony or other evidence is being offered that he or she believes is not admissible.

When the Court sustains an objection to a question, the jurors must disregard the question and the answer, if one has been given, and draw no inference from the question or answer or speculate as to what the witness would have said if permitted to answer. Jurors must also disregard evidence stricken from the record.

When the Court sustains an objection to any evidence the jurors must disregard that evidence.

When the Court overrules an objection to any evidence, the jurors must not give that evidence any more weight than if the objection had not been made.

When the evidence is completed, the attorneys will make closing arguments. These arguments are not evidence, but are given to help you evaluate the evidence. The attorneys are also permitted to argue in an attempt to persuade you to a particular verdict. You may accept or reject those arguments as you see fit.

Finally, just before you retire to consider your verdict, I will give you further instructions on the law that applies to this case.

Nita Instruction 2:01—Introduction

Members of the jury, the evidence and arguments in this case have been completed, and I will now instruct you as to the law.

The law applicable to this case is stated in these instructions, and it is your duty to follow all of them. You must not single out certain instructions and disregard others.

It is your duty to determine the facts and to determine them only from the evidence in this case. You are to apply the law to the facts and in this way decide the case. You must not be governed or influenced by sympathy or prejudice for or against any party in this case. Your verdict must be based on evidence and not on speculation, guess, or conjecture.

The evidence that you should consider consists only of witness testimony and exhibits the Court has received.

Any evidence that was received for a limited purpose should not be considered by you for any other purpose.

You should consider all the evidence in the light of your own observations and experiences in life.

Nita Instruction 2:02—Opening Statements and Closing Arguments

Opening statements are made by the attorneys to acquaint you with the facts they expect to prove. Closing arguments are made by the attorneys to discuss the facts and circumstances in the case and should be confined to the evidence and to reasonable inferences to be drawn therefrom. Neither opening statements nor closing arguments are evidence, and any statement or argument made by the attorneys that is not based on the evidence should be disregarded.

Nita Instruction 2:03—Credibility of Witnesses

You are the sole judges of the credibility of the witnesses and of the weight to be given to the testimony of each witness. In determining what credit is to be given any witness, you may take into account his ability and opportunity to observe; his manner and appearance while testifying; any interest, bias, or prejudice he may have; the reasonableness of his testimony considered in the light of all the evidence; and any other factors that bear on the believability and weight of the witness's testimony.

Nita Instruction 2:04—Burden of Proof

When I say that a party has the burden of proof on any issue or use the expression "if you find," "if you decide," or "by a preponderance of the evidence," I mean that you must be persuaded from a consideration of all the evidence in the case that the issue in question is more probably true than not true.

Any findings of fact you make must be based on probabilities, not possibilities. It may not be based on surmise, speculation, or conjecture.

JURY INSTRUCTIONS SPECIFIC TO THIS CASE

1. Introduction

The Court now will instruct you as to the claims and defenses of each party and the law governing the case. You must arrive at your verdict by applying the law, as I now instruct you, to the facts as you find them to be.

2. Background—Basic Contentions of the Parties

The parties to this case are Business Machines Incorporated, the plaintiff, and Minicom Incorporated, the defendant. BMI has sued Minicom, seeking to recover damages based on a claim that Minicom failed to pay for certain goods as required by a contract. Both sides agree that the goods were lost in transit. Minicom contends that the contract required BMI to take out insurance to protect against the loss, but that BMI failed to do so. BMI denies that the contract required it to take out insurance.

3. Damages—General

If BMI prevails, its damages will be predicated on the price of the goods that it shipped to Minicom. If Minicom prevails, its damages will be set according to the difference between the price of the goods ordered from BMI and the price of the more expensive goods it ordered from another supplier, Exrox, when the BMI parts did not arrive. Minicom also claims damages for a contract with Nieman Marcus that it allegedly lost because it had not received the BMI parts. BMI denies Minicom's claims for damages, and Minicom denies BMI's claim. I will return to this issue of damages in more detail later.

4. Existence of a Contract

You first must decide whether BMI has proven that there was a contract for the sale of the parts to Minicom. BMI has the burden of proving this issue by the preponderance of the evidence. BMI must prove all elements of the contract about which the parties do not agree. BMI must prove that there was an offer, an acceptance, and mutual assent. BMI must also prove that the goods were delivered to National Parcel Service. You must consider all facts and circumstances in deciding whether BMI made the delivery.

An offer is an expression of one's willingness to be bound by a contract. An acceptance is an expression of assent to the offer. Mutual assent occurs when an offer is communicated by one party to another and is accepted by the other party.

Whether there was mutual assent must be determined from the conduct of the parties. Whether that conduct constituted an offer and acceptance and, if it did, what its meaning was depends on what reasonable persons in the positions of the parties would have thought they meant. In determining what reasonable persons would have thought the conduct meant, you should consider the evidence as to all circumstances existing at the time of the offer or acceptance. You should not consider any different, but unexpressed meanings intended by either party.

5. Was Insurance by BMI a Term of the Contract?

If you decide that BMI proved that there was a contract between the parties for the purchase of goods from BMI by Minicom, you next must decide whether that contract included a term requiring BMI to insure the goods. Minicom has the burden of proving that term by the greater weight of the evidence. The term of insurance may be proved by showing: 1) that there was an oral contract providing for insurance; or 2) that there was a written contract for insurance. If after applying this standard you find that BMI proved a contract and Minicom did not prove a term of insurance, you will next consider BMI's damages. If you find that BMI proved a contract and Minicom proved a term of insurance you will move on to consider Minicom's damages. [If you find that neither party proved a contract, the case is ended, and you will return to the courtroom to deliver your verdict.]

6. Agency

In order for Minicom to prove an oral contract between Minicom and BMI providing for a term of insurance, Minicom must prove by the greater weight of the evidence that Virginia Young was acting as an agent of BMI on January 6, YR-1, in her telephone conversation with Michael Lubell and that she had the authority to contract for BMI. Agency is the relationship that results when one person or company, called the principal, authorizes another person, called the agent, to act for that principal. This relationship may be created by word of mouth, or by writing, or it may be implied from conduct amounting to consent or acquiescence.

A principal is liable to others for the acts of the agent in the transaction of the principal's business. In this case, to make BMI liable under the doctrine of agency for the acts of Virginia Young, Minicom must prove three things by the greater weight of the evidence:

(a) That there was a principal-agent relationship between BMI and Virginia Young on January 6, YR-1;

(b) That Virginia Young was engaged in the business of BMI at that time;

(c) That the business in which Virginia Young was engaged was within the course and scope of her employment and authority. It would be within the course and scope of her employment and authority if it was done in furtherance of the business of BMI, or if it was incidental to the duties entrusted to Virginia Young by BMI, or if it was done in carrying out a direction or an order of BMI.

7. Damages

A party injured by a breach of contract is entitled to be placed in the same position it would have occupied if the contract had been performed, insofar as this can be done by the awarding of money damages. To recover damages, the burden of proof is on the party damaged by the breach to prove by the greater weight of the evidence, first, that it sustained damages in some amount and, second, the amount of those damages.

8.   BMI's Damages

If you find that there was a contract with no term of insurance, you must award BMI the price of the goods, plus shipping and interest, as required by the contract, since Minicom has agreed that the contract called for payment of that amount and no payment has been made. If, however, you find that contract had a term requiring BMI to insure, Minicom is the party injured by the breach, and BMI recovers nothing.

9.   Minicom's Damages

If you find that it was a term of the contract that BMI would insure the goods, you must decide if Minicom was injured by BMI's breach in failing to insure, i.e., whether Minicom made a reasonable purchase of goods from Exrox in substitution for those due from BMI and that Minicom did so in good faith and without unreasonable delay. If you find that Minicom did this, Minicom is entitled to recover the difference between the cost of the substituted goods from Exrox and its cost under the original contract with BMI.

Minicom also makes a further claim for consequential loss—that it lost a contract with Nieman Marcus because of BMI's breach of contract. You must decide whether Minicom has proven, by the greater weight of the evidence, a) that it had a contract with Neiman Marcus, b) that it lost profits on that contract because of BMI's failure to insure the shipment, and c) the amount of the profits, if any, that Minicom lost on such contract.

IN THE SUPERIOR COURT

IN AND FOR THE COUNTY OF DARROW AND STATE OF NITA

BUSINESS MACHINES INCORPORATED,)
Plaintiff,   )
)   CIVIL ACTION
)   YR-1:2342
v.   )
)
MINICOM INCORPORATED,   )
Defendant.   )
)

SPECIAL VERDICT FORM #1

We, the jury, and each of us finds:

1.   For the plaintiff in the amount of $_____.

2.   For the defendant in the amount of $_____.

[You may answer either question 1 or question 2, but not both.]

Date   Foreperson

IN THE SUPERIOR COURT

IN AND FOR THE COUNTY OF DARROW AND STATE OF NITA

BUSINESS MACHINES INCORPORATED,   )
)
Plaintiff,   )   CIVIL ACTION
)   YR-1:2342
v.   )
)
MINICOM INCORPORATED,   )
)
Defendant.   )

SPECIAL VERDICT FORM #2

PART I

1. Did BMI prove a contract existed between BMI and Minicom for the sale of 100 gross of ICP-73s, that BMI delivered the goods to NPS, and that Minicom failed to pay for the goods? Yes _____ No _____

If your answer is no, skip the rest of Part I and all of Part II. You should move on to answer Part III. If your answer is yes, please answer the following question:

2. Did Minicom prove that the contract required BMI to insure the goods before shipment and that BMI failed to do so? Yes _____ No _____

If your answer is no, please answer the questions in Part II.

If your answer is yes, skip Part II and Part III and answer the questions in Part IV.

PART II

1. What amount of damages has BMI proven? Enter the amount in dollars: $_____.

This concludes your deliberations. If your verdict on each of the questions you have answered is unanimous, have the foreperson sign the verdict form.

PART III

1. Has Minicom proven that Virginia Young was an agent of BMI for the purpose of entering into contracts?[1] Yes _____ No _____

If your answer is no, this concludes your deliberations. If your verdict on each of the questions is unanimous, have the foreperson sign the verdict form.

If your answer is yes, please answer the following question:

1. Did Minicom prove that a contract existed between BMI and Minicom for the sale of 100 gross ICP-73s, that BMI was required to insure the goods before shipment, that BMI failed to do so, and that Minicom never received the goods? Yes _____ No _____

If your answer is no, this concludes your deliberations. If your verdict on each of the questions you have answered is unanimous, have the foreperson sign the verdict form.

If your answer is yes, please answer the questions in Part IV.

PART IV

1. What amount of damages has Minicom proven? Enter the amount in dollars. $_____

This concludes your deliberations. If your verdict in each of the questions you have answered is unanimous, have the foreperson sign the verdict form.

IN THIS VERDICT EACH OF US CONCURS.

Date   Foreperson

---

1. This section need only be asked if the theory of recovery for Minicom is that a verbal contract was entered into between Lubell and Young during the telephone conversations between them.

IN THE SUPERIOR COURT

IN AND FOR THE COUNTY OF DARROW AND STATE OF NITA

BUSINESS MACHINES INCORPORATED,	)	
	)	
Plaintiff,	)	CIVIL ACTION
	)	YR-1:2342
v.	)	
	)	
MINICOM INCORPORATED,	)	
	)	
Defendant.	)	

SPECIAL VERDICT FORM #3[2]

PART I

Did Minicom prove by a preponderance of the evidence that the contract required BMI to insure the goods before shipment? Yes _____ No _____

If your answer to Part I is no, proceed to Part II. Do not consider Part III. If your answer to Part I is yes, proceed to Part III. Do not consider Part II.

PART II

What amount of damages has BMI proven by a preponderance of the evidence? Enter the amount in dollars. $_____.

PART III

What amount of damages has Minicom proven by a preponderance of the evidence? Enter the amount in dollars. $_____.

IN THIS VERDICT EACH OF US CONCURS.

Date   Foreperson

_____

2. For use when the parties have stipulated the existence of a contract, but the term of insurance is still an issue.